The Power of
3:00AM
and the
Mystery of the Watches

J. E. Charles

Copyright Permission
**The Power of 3:00AM and the
Mystery of the Watches and Seasons**
© 2020 J.E Charles
A publication of Dunamis Christian Center |
Upper Room Fire Prayer Ministry
P.O Box 12352 Pleasanton CA 94588
Printed in the United States of America

All rights reserved. No part of this publication may be reproduced, stored in a retrieval system or be transmitted in any form or by any means, mechanical, electronic, photocopying or otherwise without prior written consent of the publisher.

Unless otherwise noted, Scripture quotations are taken from the New King James Version (NKJV). Copyright © 1979, 1980, 1982 by Thomas Nelson, Inc. Used by permission. All rights reserved.

Scripture quotations designated KJV are from the King James Version of the Holy Bible. Scripture quotations designated NASB or NASB95 are from the New American Standard Bible, © the Lockman Foundation 1960, 1962, 1963, 1968, 1971, 1972, 1973, 1975, 1977, 1995.

Scripture quotations marked (NLT) are taken from the Holy Bible, New Living Translation, copyright © 1996, 2004, 2007 by Tyndale House Foundation. Used by permission of Tyndale House Publishers, Inc., Carol Stream, IL 60188. All rights reserved. Scripture quotations marked ESV are from The Holy Bible, English Standard Version® (ESV®), copyright © 2001 by Crossway, a publishing ministry of Good News Publishers. Used by permission. All rights reserved.

Scripture quotations marked The Message are taken from The Message. The Bible in Contemporary English, Copyright © 1993, 1994, 1995, 1996, 2000, 2001, 2002. Used by permission of NavPress Publishing Group.

Products are available at special quantity discounts for bulk purchase for sales promotion, premium's, fund-raising, and educational needs.

For details contact us at P. O Box 12352, Pleasanton CA 94588 or www.dunamisbookstore.com, Email: sales@upperroomfireprayer.org or Call 408 508 4304

Library of Congress Cataloging in-Publication Data: An application to register this book for cataloging has been submitted to the Library of Congress.

International Standard Book Number:
ISBN: 978-1-7362288-2-1

Contents

Acknowledgements... v
Introduction.. vii
Dedication ix

Part 1: Overview

Chapter 1   The Watchmen and Their Watchtowers... 1
Chapter 2   Enemies at The Gate.............................. 12
Chapter 3   It's Time to Rise Up!.............................. 20

Part 2: Unraveling the Mysteries of the Night Watches

Chapter 4   The First Watch (6 p.m.-9 p.m.) 33
Chapter 5   The Second Watch (9 p.m.-Noon) 40
Chapter 6   The Third Watch (Midnight-3 a.m.)...... 45
Chapter 7   The Fourth Watch (3 a.m.-6 a.m.)......... 50
Chapter 8   Command the Morning 57
Chapter 9   Early Riser Confessions for Ministers..... 76

PART 3: UNRAVELING THE MYSTERIES OF THE DAY WATCHES

Chapter 10   The First Day Watch (6 a.m.-9 a.m.)...... 83
Chapter 11   The Second Day Watch (9 a.m.-Noon).. 88
Chapter 12   The Third Day Watch (Noon-3 p.m.).... 97
Chapter 13   The Fourth Day Watch (3 p.m.-6 p.m.) 103

PART 4: UNRAVELING THE MYSTERIES OF THE SEASONS OF POWER

Chapter 14   Solstice..113
Chapter 15   Summer Solstice—A Time for Work 118
Chapter 16   Winter Solstice—Harvest Time........... 121
Chapter 17   Equinox—A Balanced Life 124
Chapter 18   Autumnal Equinox—When Things Fall Apart 128
Chapter 19   Spring Equinox—A New Thing 131
Chapter 20   Command the Seasons 134

Author Information..141
More books from J.E Charles 144

Acknowledgements

I Hereby acknowledge the contributions of all men of God, whom God has used in the past and who are still being used by God to prepare me for the coming of our Lord Jesus Christ.

Furthermore, I hereby acknowledge Dr. D.K. Olukoya, an apostle and prophet of God who understands the power of persistent prayer, whose ministry has seriously blessed my family and revolutionized the act of prayer in our generation. May the Lord keep them 'til the day of His coming.

I salute my wonderful wife, Lady Akuss, for her invaluable support in the ministry. I appreciate her unquantifiable love and support.

Introduction

The Eastman Kodak Company, founded in 1888, was for most of its history one of the most prosperous companies in the world. Its dominance in the photographic film industry was so great that the phrase "a Kodak moment" became part of our daily vernacular to refer to any moment that deserved to be captured on film. But in 2012 Kodak filed for bankruptcy and in 2020 its stock price reached a low of $1.59 per share.

What happened? *Digital* photography. Kodak failed to recognize and adapt to the new technology and paid the price.

It's important to recognize the times in which one lives. It can mean the difference between success and failure, life and death. Jesus said to the people of Jerusalem,

> *"For the days shall come upon thee, that thine enemies shall cast a trench about thee, and compass thee round, and keep thee in on every side, And shall lay thee even with the ground, and thy children within thee; and they shall not leave in thee one stone*

> *upon another; **because thou knewest not the time of thy visitation.***" (Luke 19:43-44, emphasis added)

Jesus said destruction was coming upon them because they failed to recognize the *"time"* of his coming. Jesus also, in Matthew 16:3, rebuked the people for not being able to *"discern the signs of the times."*

I have written this book to help you discern the various times and seasons in life. In Biblical days, the different time periods of each day were divided into distinct *watches* that called for particular behaviors. Likewise, in creation God has placed separate seasons that call for unique activities to be performed.

Recognizing these *"signs of the times"* is key to our fulfillment in life, to our realizing God's great plan for us. I present to you *The Mysteries of the Watches of Prayer and the Seasons of Power* to help you recognize these times and to know how you should respond to them to enjoy God's blessings.

> *"I counsel thee to … anoint thine eyes with eyesalve, that thou mayest see."* (Revelation 3:18)

Dedication

To the person of the Holy Spirit,
Who is the very reason for my being
And
To my children, living Faith and Ike,
who should carry this message of the gospel
of Christ to their generation.

PART 1
OVERVIEW

THE WATCHMEN AND THEIR WATCHTOWERS

And there stood a watchman on the tower in Jezreel, and he spied the company of Jehu as he came, and said, I see a company. And Joram said, Take an horseman, and send to meet them, and let him say, Is it peace? So there went one on horseback to meet him, and said, Thus saith the king, Is it peace?

2 Kings 9:17-18 (emphasis added)

In the passage above, we see the function of a *watchman* on his *tower* (I will use the word *watchman* in this book to follow the Biblical text, but I don't mean to be gender-specific; the truths I will reveal from Scripture apply to men and women!). We see that a watchman was a guard or lookout posted on a tower at the gates of the city, in this case the city of *Jezreel*. His job was to point out any potential danger approaching the city.

The watchman in our text was doing his duty, so when

Jehu came to execute the prophecies of divine vengeance against Jezebel and the house of wicked King Ahab, he was quickly spotted from a distance. The watchman then alerted everyone that Jehu was coming. Practically speaking, Jehu was a divinely-ordained angel of judgment and death, but he was not able to carry out a surprise attack against Jezreel because a watchman spotted him and alerted the city. That's how powerful and important a watchman (or watch*woman*) is!

Instinctively, we know how important it is to secure our treasures and territories, but what's the use of a gate without a guard to secure it, and what's the benefit of a watchtower without someone to mount watch on it?

What It Means to Keep Watch!

> *"Watch ye therefore, and pray always, that ye may be accounted worthy to escape all these things that shall come to pass, and to stand before the Son of man."* (Luke 21:36)

The command to *watch* is featured twenty-nine times in the New Testament! And in Mathew and Luke, we find four instances when the Lord Jesus himself taught us to "Watch and pray!"

In addition, the Apostle Paul instructed believers to *pray without ceasing* (1 Thessalonians 5:17). These New

Testament instructions make it clear that as a Christian, you should strive to be spiritually alert and awake!

Jesus' words in Luke 21:36 in the above text tell us that we need to *"watch"* and *"pray"* so that we can *"escape"* from various things. In other words, there are threats that lurk around the realm and terrain of the spirit. We need to understand that we're in the flesh, but not of the flesh! There are spiritual dimensions and realities that interfere with and influence our lives. We cannot afford a moment of carelessness until we reach our home, the safe haven of heaven!

As long as we're in the flesh, we must watch and pray ALWAYS! You see, keeping watch is done on the platform—i.e., watchtower—of rugged discipline and effective prayer.

So the first secret we have to establish here is that when you pray, you're watching in the spirit realm—keeping the enemy at bay! And since the devil, our adversary, is roaming about everywhere like a lion seeking whom he may devour (1 Peter 5:8), we cannot stop watching; we must not stop praying! Praying without ceasing, continuously, every hour of the day and the night, makes every moment valuable and powerful. Every hour in life is meant to be a watch (or prayer) hour.

GIRD YOUR LOINS, KEEP YOUR LIGHT BURNING

The Lord Jesus said in Luke 12:35: *"Let your loins be girded about, and your lights burning."*

The *"loins"* speak of the flesh, our natural tendencies and affinity for pleasure, our lack of interest in spiritual things. But our Lord tells us here what to do with the flesh: *"Let [it] be girded about,"* that is, disciplined and self-controlled.

But in addition to girding our loins, and just as important, we must keep our light burning bright and hot! *Light* speaks of revelation, insights dropped into our spirit by the Spirit of God. In fact, the light of the *Spirit himself* lives in our heart, giving us a dynamic relationship with our Creator. You see, discipline without revelation leads only to failure and frustration. Just think of the Pharisees; no one was more disciplined than they, but they had no light, no joy in their heart, and in the end turned into murderers of the Son of God. There's nothing more common in our world today than folks engaged in hard work without revelation. King Solomon said, the labor of fools wearies them! When you battle depression, you need to question your access to revelation. When was the last time you heard from God? Beloved, you may not need more hard work; you may need to sit under a good sermon by your pastor. God said, my people are destroyed not only because they sleep on their watches, but also because they watch and work without light.

Tithe Your Nights and Fast Your Sleep

True spiritual discipline will result in light. When it comes to watching and praying, we need to understand that it is another form of fasting and praying. How many of us like to tithe our nights and fast our sleep? No, it's not the same as being fast asleep! It's to give a portion of your night to God, not because you have to (because you don't; it won't make God love and accept you any more than he already does), but because you want to keep that light burning.

I believe God wants us to learn to tithe the night, to fast our sleep. For example, you might tithe your sleep by saying, "I will stay awake from midnight till 3:00 a.m. tonight watching and praying." But do so with wisdom, not overpromising what you can or truly will do.

Just as you should be wise when it comes to your choice of food when you're fasting, when you are fasting *and watching*, you don't want to eat heavy hamburgers or McDonald's; you want to eat light food, such as salad greens, so that you don't put your body to sleep. To watch and pray, your body must feel healthy and light.

Watching and Waiting on Purpose

When you understand the purpose of watching and waiting, you'll be motivated to sustain that posture until you experience manifestations of the promise.

Jesus, after telling us to gird our loins and keep our

lights burning, went on to tell us why: *"And ye yourselves like unto men that wait for their lord, when he will return from the wedding; that when he cometh and knocketh, they may open unto him immediately"* (Luke 12:36, emphasis added). He said the purpose for watching and waiting was to be ready to open the door when the Lord knocks! To be ready to pray and intercede when the Lord leads us to.

Shirley Dobson, wife of Dr. James Dobson of Focus on the Family, told about a time when her husband was away on a trip and she was home with their young children. She said, "One night about 2:00 a.m., I awoke with a start. I was afraid and didn't know why. For a few minutes (it seemed like hours!), I lay in bed worrying. Finally, I forced myself out of bed and sank to my knees. 'Oh, Lord,' I prayed, 'I don't know why I'm so frightened. I ask you to watch over our home and to protect our family. Send your guardian angel to be with us.'"

Then she climbed back in bed and fell asleep. The next morning their teen-aged babysitter ran over and told her there'd been a robbery in the neighborhood last night: the Dobson's next-door neighbors had their vacation money stolen, about $500. It had happened about 2:00 a.m.—the time Shirley had awakened. Shirley thought, *If a burglar wanted to break in our house*—she knew the window he would try, one hidden by a hedge. They went to look at it, and saw that the screen was bent and the sill splintered. Someone had indeed tried to break in!

The police told Shirley that if the burglar really wanted to get in, he would have. Something had stopped him. Shirley was convinced it was her prayer.

We need to watch and wait so we can be ready when the Lord calls on us, ready to pray and intercede.

Jesus went on to say in Luke 12:37: *"Blessed are those servants, whom the lord when he cometh shall find watching."* You see, every believer is a servant of God. When we respond to God's command to watch, we position ourselves in a place where he can find us faithful and worthy of the glory and power that he is pouring out in these last days before his return.

Just as the blessing of spiritual alertness enabled Elisha to go from being an ordinary farmer to a man of power and influence in Israel, so you can be transformed as you stay alert for divine intervention. And when Elisha asked for a double portion of the power and glory in Elijah's ministry, there was only one requirement: "Will you watch?" Elijah asked! Elijah knew that blessings, glory, and power are for neither sleepers nor gluttons. When a sleeper gets glory, it's only a matter of time before he loses it to the enemy. And as for a glutton, rather than hungering and thirsting for righteousness and the divine presence, he'll trade it all for a sweet taste and a vain pleasure.

On the other hand, watchers are men and women who earn, and keep, God's glory for unusual manifestations in their life, their family, their mission, their ministry, and their career.

The Bible says that strength is given to men and women who guard their gates day and night. Here is the amazing promise that Jesus made to those who stay watchful and ready to open their door to the Lord: *"Blessed are those servants, whom the lord when he cometh shall find watching: verily I say unto you, that he shall gird himself, and make them to sit down to meat, and will come forth and serve them"* (Luke 12:37). Beloved, God cannot lie! When Elohim says that he will come down to serve those whom he finds waiting for him, you don't need to doubt it for one second! Spiritually, in this present reality, that symbolizes divine visitations that trigger supernatural manifestations in our lives. When God visits you, he'll bless you *beyond your expectations and the waiting and watchful season will be treasurable to you beyond measure!*

Maintain the Watcher's Posture

Jesus' priceless teaching in Luke 12 continues with these words:

> *"And if he shall come **in the second watch**, or come **in the third watch**, and find them so, blessed are those servants. And this know, that if the goodman of the house had known what hour the thief would come, he would have watched, and not have suffered his house to be broken through. Be ye therefore*

ready also: for the Son of man cometh at an hour when ye think not." (38-40, emphasis added)

Jesus tells us to always keep watch, for we do not know the hour when our Lord may come. He specifically mentions watching *"in the second watch"* and *"the third watch."* What did the second watch and the third watch refer to? The Romans in those days divided the night into four watches. The first watch is 6-9 p.m., the second watch is 9 p.m.-Midnight, and the third watch is Midnight-3 a.m.

So, again, the third watch is Midnight-3 a.m. and the second watch is 9 p.m.-Midnight. Now with this understanding, consider carefully what I say in the following section.

Mount Your Watchtower!

Since prayer is the platform for spiritual engagement, it is your watchtower, the place from where you detect and destroy demonic infiltrations into your life. Hence, as a Christian, the most important thing that you should be conscious of is the integrity and intensity of your prayers, of your time on the watchtower. In the Bible, prayer is the way we keep watch over our lives and the lives of others.

Again, I need to remind you that Jesus is at the right hand of the Father, saying to you, "My child, watch and pray." The watcher is useless until he climbs his watchtower because he lacks the vantage point of the raised platform. We are useless until we climb the watchtower of prayer and gain the divine elevation that keeps the enemy under surveillance and judgment!

So it appears prayer cannot be effective without watching, because when we pray we mount up with wings like eagles to realms of glory that the enemy cannot comprehend.

You see, prayer time is supposed to be a time when a Christian is at alert. In this sense, prayer is like a force that awakens the spirit of a man, keeps him at alert as to what is going on in his environment, both his physical environment and the spiritual environment. Hence the need to take a stand on the watchtower of life.

This book is for you if you desire to detect and terminate your adversary. It's for you if you hate unpleasant surprises! Keep reading if you want to enroll in God's school of prayer and mount the tower of power! This book will bring revival to you and break the spirit of spiritual slumber over your life.

Are you ready?

PRAYERS (PRAY THESE PRAYERS WITH ME, BELOVED)

- Every demonic door opened against me, every demonic portal opened against me, I close them right now by the power of the blood of Jesus.

- Every counterfeit cord, every ley line drawn against my dwelling, drawn against my properties, drawn against my body, drawn against my soul, drawn against my spirit line, with the Bible in my hand serving as a sword, I cut and burn the silver cord, I cut and burn the ley line.
- Every transfer of spirit, every fragment of Satan in my body and home, I bind and cast you out now by the power of the blood of Jesus.

ENEMIES AT THE GATE

*Be sober, be vigilant;
because your adversary the devil,
as a roaring lion, walketh about, seeking whom he may devour.*

1 Peter 5:8

We are often told that experience is the best teacher. When men of experience give warnings, we are enjoined to take them seriously. The Apostle Peter, in the text above, was speaking from his experience on the watchtower of life. Do you remember when he failed to watch with Jesus in the Garden of Gethsemane? The Bible says,

> *And he cometh unto the disciples, and findeth them asleep, and saith unto Peter, What, could ye not watch with me one hour?*

> *Watch and pray, that ye enter not into temptation: the spirit indeed is willing, but the flesh is weak.*
>
> Matthew 26:40-41

Did Peter heed this warning at the time? No. And what happened? He ended up denying the Lord three times; that is, he fell victim to the enemies at the gate. Peter would have perished in the hands of the adversary, the devil, but he quickly retraced his steps, took possession of his gate, and watched perpetually. So years later, he could look back and write: There's an enemy at your gate (the prowling lion Satan) and you need to be vigilant.

The Bible tells us, *"The thief cometh not, but for to steal, and to kill, and to destroy"* (John 10:10).

Have you seen a lion stalk its prey? Slowly, but steadily, it moves in and pounces. Most times, the prey has little to no chance of escape. However, the lion does not come close to the devil in stalking prowess. The devil has mastered and refined the art of subtlety.

Let us connect the dots. The devil is loitering around the gate—the entrance—to your life. You are the at-alert watchman and fearless gatekeeper who needs to spot the enemy. The devil is aiming for the gate to gain an entrance into your life in order to release future-distorting and life-damaging havoc. Do you know why the gate is important? Let's take a cue from warfare.

In ancient warfare, the city gate was key; whoever

controlled it had the strategic advantage. Both sides therefore strove to take control of the gate. Whoever controlled the gate could control the fate of their opponent; as soon as the adversary gained power at the gate, the city must fall. There are several ancient wars that were fought and won because the enemy gained access or control of the gates of a city. Possessing the gates means you are able to divert resources away from the city to create starvation and force surrender.

But when it comes to the gate to your life, the *gate* is not a physical gate but a place, position, period, time, or season, which gives you an advantage over someone or something. Possessing the gate can be the difference between life and death, which is why the devil aims for the gate to your life. If the gate is such a destiny-defining thing, you must be wide awake at every rustle in the bush.

When the enemy is at your gate, you feel hemmed in on every side—east, west, north, south—and it seems the very air you breathe was sent to spy on you. You sense the hair on your back standing straight up, your pulse beating fast, your eyes wide open, and your fists ready to deal a blow. Then, you know it is not a time to slumber or sleep. It is a time for self-denial—denial of sleep, food, pleasure—and a time to watch and pray to ensure that you remain in control of the gate!

While you are watching, the enemy is working. While you are praying, the enemy is plotting. The devil is implacable! He is constantly and consistently tracking your next move and planning your downfall. He is looking for the perfect time—the right *watch*—to aim and shoot you down once and for all. Everything that matters to you in life, that gives you a reason for existence, can be stolen and destroyed in the blink of an eye. Therefore, you must not let down your guard!

The Link to The Gate

Why do you think the devil is constantly *roaming,* according to Peter? He's looking for your blind spot, your weakness, your frailty, and your unguarded hour. He is scanning for the particular *watch* in which you are most vulnerable to attack and capture. In short, he is looking for your weakest link—the link to you gate. The truth is, your gate is only as secure as its weakest link.

The Great Wall of China is the longest structure ever built, stretching (with all its lengths) about 4,500 miles—about 2,000 miles longer than the distance between New York City and L.A. Some parts of the wall are as high as 35 feet, and as thick as 25 feet. It was all built by hand. It was built to protect the Chinese from barbarian hordes, yet during the first 100 years of the wall's existence, China was successfully invaded three times.

How were they invaded? Well, the barbarians never scaled or broke down the wall. They simply bribed a gatekeeper and marched right in through an open door!

Beloved, your gate is only as secure as your weakest

link. You're the watcher at your gate, its king. Is the city safe when you're on duty? Are you sleeping when you should be watching your fortress? Are you lounging in your bed when you should be fighting against your enemies?

Sunset at Midday

The danger of sleeping on your watch is illustrated by the Old Testament story of Ishbosheth. After the death of King Saul and Jonathan his firstborn son, Ishbosheth, another son of Saul, became king. Abner, Saul's army commander, became the new king's bodyguard. This was at the same time when David was made king in Judah. There was tension between David's army and the warriors of Ishbosheth. The control and reign of all Israel was at stake.

Luckily for Ishbosheth, David was a man who feared the Lord and was not going to attack Ishbosheth just to secure the throne. David was waiting on God to bring all Israel under his reign without actively deploying military might against Ishbosheth. This good man considered usurping power an unrighteous thing to do.

However, he needed not to worry about Ishbosheth, because a spoiled prince, become king, will not last. Ishbosheth's error: refusal to watch and inability to submit to his watchman, Abner. For a just cause, Ishbosheth challenged Abner for sleeping with one of King Saul's concubines. This was a legitimate accusation because it seemed like treason; however, Ishbosheth was ill-prepared to take charge of his territory. He had not mastered the art of alertness and watch-keeping.

Consider what the Bible says about Ishbosheth:

> [1] *And when Saul's son [Ishbosheth] heard that Abner was dead in Hebron, his hands were feeble, and all the Israelites were troubled....*
>
> [5] *And the sons of Rimmon the Beerothite, Rechab and Baanah, went, and came about the heat of the day to the house of Ishbosheth, who lay on a bed **at noon**.*
>
> [6] *And they came thither into the midst of the house, as though they would have fetched wheat; and they smote him under the fifth rib: and Rechab and Baanah his brother escaped.*
>
> [7] *For when they came into the house, **he lay on his bed** in his bedchamber, and they smote him, and slew him, and beheaded him, and took his head, and gat them away through the plain all night.*
>
> - 2 Samuel 4:1, 5-7 (emphasis added)

Abner died because he defected to David; some of David's men felt threatened, so they killed him. This news caused great panic in Israel and within Ishbosheth's camp. Yet the naïve king did not respond appropriately by securing his territory. Mind you, David could have let him keep part of the kingdom if he was able to sustain the position. Remember, he that controls the gates retains the treasures.

I believe some of Ishbosheth's soldiers felt they needed to show loyalty to David, so they decided to kill Ishbosheth. And sadly, they succeeded! They saw the loophole, they knew his weakness. The boys knew their king neither watched nor cared about watchers. He lived carelessly in a place and time of intense conflict. And unfortunately, but not surprisingly, he was burned!

In fact, the enemy is known to show up and challenge us when we least expect it, and that's what happened with Ishbosheth. He was sleeping during the noon watch, the text above reveals; that is, he was sleeping during the period of the day reserved for heightened activity. This was a time for the king to tend to the affairs of the state. But Ishbosheth was sleeping while death lurked. He had already gotten a warning sign.

And what did the enemies at the gate do? They snuck in and took the king's life.

Ishbosheth failed to take the responsibilities that came with being at the gate of power. As a king, he failed to protect his throne. As a father, he failed to protect his home.

To keep watch is as important as one's life. Spiritually, it requires alertness in prayer. It also requires honoring men and women that the Lord has set over you as watchmen. Not like adulterous Abner, but as righteous shepherds over your soul.

Your enemies want to take control of your gate and steal your gold, and once they succeed, they leave you one of the living-dead. To avert this danger, you must watch your gate. If you keep watch, you will not only avert the dangers to you, but will provide security to others within the sphere of your influence.

God Bless You!

Prayers

- I pull down every evil alter erected against my destiny in the name of Jesus. I destroy such altars by fire and thunder!
- Every inherited infirmity, you are a liar; die and perish in the name of Jesus.
- Any man or woman that takes the form of an animal—an insect, snake, bird—because of me, you shall not return to your original body; therefore I cast you into the pit in the name of Jesus.
- I call upon the mighty angels with swords, I call upon the army of heaven to surround me, and to now attack any demonic power above, below, and around me.

3

IT'S TIME TO RISE UP!

*"Hast thou commanded the morning since thy days;
and caused the dayspring to know his place; That it might take hold
of the ends of the earth, that the wicked might be shaken out of it?"*

Job 38:12, 13

"Rrrrrring!" Your alarm is ringing! Wake up! Listen! It's time to take action! There are times you have to wake up at night to perform some preset task, attend to some emergency or impromptu job, or solve a pressing or nagging problem. You want to be sleeping, right? But you can't, not when your house is on fire and things are getting messy. Problems and issues are the alarm clocks of life, sending a warning signal, sending a jolt to your senses and rousing you from sleep. You've got to do something before the situation escalates and gets out of control!

Jesus both comforts and warns in his words recorded

in John 16:33: *"In the world ye shall have tribulation: but be of good cheer; I have overcome the world."* (John 16:33). The comfort: No matter what comes, we can have peace in him. The warning: There shall be *"tribulation"* in our lives—troubles and challenges—and as a matter of urgency, we must rise early to the occasion to watch and intercede.

You must have an always-on approach to every situation. Why? You'll be able to detect a slight change in your spiritual temperature, a looming storm in your marriage, a potential evil in the church, and more. Your responsibility as a watchman is to have your eyes on your environment; your elevated spiritual vantage point offers you a rare chance to have an eagle-eyed view and to make perceptive decisions. Therefore, it's time to wake up to the reality of what's at stake.

In our modern world, there's a system in place in almost every sector to monitor what's going on: an early warning system to tip off a brewing storm, a financial tracking system to monitor the stock market, a thermometer to measure body temperature, and CCTVs in the supermarket. We need the same in our lives! Therefore, watchman, it's time to rise. The enemy might be plotting a coup. It's time to intercede for your family, business, country, and church. It's time to nip the approaching attack in the bud before it gets to you! It's time to rise up and watch!

Your Family

You're a watchman over your family. A whole lot is going on that needs your intercession. The stability and success of your marriage, the security of your home, a beautiful future for your kids, your and your spouse's job security; all require your *watch*. You need to eke out a place for your family, stake a claim to what's rightfully yours, and fight to keep it.

Jacob did exactly all of this, as we read in Genesis 32:

> [22] *And he rose up that night, and took his two wives, and his two womenservants, and his eleven sons, and passed over the ford Jabbok.*
>
> [23] *And he took them, and sent them over the brook, and sent over that he had.*
>
> [24] *And Jacob was left alone; and there wrestled a man with him until the breaking of the day.*
>
> [25] *And when he saw that he prevailed not against him, he touched the hollow of his thigh; and the hollow of Jacob's thigh was out of joint, as he wrestled with him.*

> [26] *And he said, Let me go, for the day breaketh. And he said, I will not let thee go, except thou bless me."*

The future of Jacob's family was at stake. Esau, his brother was coming to meet him with 400 armed soldiers. Jacob saw the storm approaching and knew that it was now or never. What did he do? He set his *watch!* He did away with all forms of hindrance—his wife, children, servants, livestock—in order to save them.

You see, if you will save your family, you must put away from you whatever hinders you from keeping watch, be it time with your loved-ones or your own pursuits. The truth is, if you don't take this stand, you may end up losing all. Jesus said, *"For whosoever will save his life shall lose it: and whosoever will lose his life for my sake shall find it"* (Matthew 16:25). It sounds counterintuitive, but if you will stay true to your solemn pledge as a watchman, you must be ready to give what it takes.

Jacob put his life on the line to save his family. The Bible said he was *left alone.* He was alone in the cold moonlit night, with the eastern sky dazzling with stars. Like a man staring into the dark before him, Jacob didn't know what was coming for him, but as every watchman should be, he was prepared.

Jacob entered into spiritual warfare in the fourth *watch* (between 3-6 a.m.) to gain control of his gate and intercede for his family. He remembered God's promises to Abraham and Isaac, and how his father had blessed him. Here he had reached the decisive moment in his life, when he was really going to take what rightfully belonged to him. It didn't come easy, nor was it without a fatality. However, what's important is that he got what he wanted: the blessings of Abraham. As we see in the following verses from Genesis 32:

> ^{27} *And he said unto him, What is thy name? And he said, Jacob.*
>
> ^{28} *And he said, Thy name shall be called no more Jacob, but Israel: for as a prince hast thou power with God and with men, and hast prevailed.*
>
> ^{29} *And Jacob asked him, and said, Tell me, I pray thee, thy name. And he said, Wherefore is it that thou dost ask after my name? And he blessed him there.*
>
> ^{30} *And Jacob called the name of the place Peniel: for I have seen God face to face, and my life is preserved.*

Jacob's life was not only preserved, but his posterity was secured and preserved. By the time morning broke, Jacob walked into a new dawn. Now he was not going to enjoy the rewards alone, but his future generations would continue to benefit from his purpose and his determination to keep his *watch* and secure his *gate*.

The Church

In Acts 12, we have an intriguing account of a mass attack by a group of fierce watchmen. Sometimes, the number matters! Mathematically, a task that requires one man one hour will take seven men only about eight and a half minutes to complete. Some of life's issues require a solitary intercession as in the case of Jacob, while others require a swarm of intercessors, an army.

Like army ants aggressively attack in numbers, the disciples interceded for Peter with a burning passion. The killing of James was the alarm signal the church needed to wake up, but it wasn't sufficient for them to keep *watch* until Herod nabbed Peter—the leader of the nascent group—with the intent of killing him, too.

Herod was the enemy at the *gate* of the church, and Peter was its lead watchman. Remember, when the leader is taken, the followers become prey. However, Herod mistook Peter's easy arrest as a sign of weakness of the church. What he didn't know was that the church had many watchmen who were wielding the serious weapon of prayer.

> *Peter therefore was kept in prison: but prayer was made without ceasing of the church unto God for him.* (Acts 12:5)

All of which meant that Herod, the *intruder* at the *gate,* was in for trouble! The disciples rallied together at the house of John Mark's mother and started the fire of prayer. It was a pivotal moment, the result of which would alter the course of history. If the church failed to pray and Peter was killed, the destiny of the future church was in danger, the destiny of believers like you and me. Much hung in the balance!

Just as it happened with Jacob, the disciples prayed through the night until the answer came in the fourth watch. You can see that the fourth watch is highly significant. It was the hour of deliverance for the Israelites at the Red Sea (Exodus 14:27 – called morning watch); Jesus walked on the water during the fourth watch to deliver his disciples from the storm (Matthew 14:25). At this same hour, the angel of God came to Peter's deliverance in Acts 12:

> [7] *And, behold, the angel of the Lord came upon him, and a light shined in the prison: and he smote Peter on the side, and raised him up, saying, Arise up quickly. And his chains fell off from his hands.*

> [8] *And the angel said unto him, Gird thyself, and bind on thy sandals. And so he did. And he saith unto him, Cast thy garment about thee, and follow me.*
>
> [9] *And he went out, and followed him; and wist not that it was true which was done by the angel; but thought he saw a vision.*
>
> [10] *When they were past the first and the second ward, they came unto the iron gate that leadeth unto the city; which opened to them of his own accord: and they went out, and passed on through one street; and forthwith the angel departed from him.*
>
> [11] *And when Peter was come to himself, he said, Now I know of a surety, that the Lord hath sent his angel, and hath delivered me out of the hand of Herod, and from all the expectation of the people of the Jews.*

God has given unlimited and unstoppable power to the church. He said, *"Verily I say unto you, Whatsoever ye shall bind on earth shall be bound in heaven: and whatsoever ye shall loose on earth shall be loosed in heaven"* (Mark 18:18). This power rests in the hands of watchmen who control the *gate.* They wield it to stop the onslaught of the enemy and deliver men from the jaws of evil.

A Job Opening

There's a "Help Wanted" sign in the window of heaven. God is looking for men who will keep *watch*.

> *"And I sought for a man among them, that should make up the hedge, and stand in the gap before me for the land, that I should not destroy it: but I found none."* (Ezekiel 22:30)

> *Therefore he said that he would destroy them, had not Moses his chosen stood before him in the breach, to turn away his wrath, lest he should destroy them.* (Psalm 106:23)

Will you be among the watchmen who will rise up and pray for their family, their nation, and the church? It is a noble calling and a key assignment. The destinies of nations rest on your shoulders. Therefore, hear the sound of the bell, hear the alarm: It's time to rise up and *watch*.

Prayers

- I drag all the enemies of marriage to the court of the Almighty. Let God arise in the Name of Jesus and judge them by fire.

- ou unfavorable friends, I drag you to the court of the Almighty. Let God arise in the Name of Jesus and judge them by fire.

PART 2
UNRAVELING THE MYSTERIES OF THE NIGHT WATCHES

THE FIRST WATCH
(6 P.M.-9 P.M.)

Arise, cry out in the night: in the beginning of the watches pour out thine heart like water before the face of the Lord: lift up thy hands toward him for the life of thy young children, that faint for hunger in the top of every street.

Lamentations 2:19 (emphasis added)

The world we live in is full of evil and pain. We are often faced with challenges and battles as we journey through life. The devil is always out to ensure that nothing good and meaningful comes our way, no matter how much we strive. He is relentlessly waging war against God's children. Thus, as believers, we must understand that there is a need to always be on the alert if we hope to win our spiritual battles and succeed in life.

The lens through which we view life matters and is fundamental to our survival. You must understand that

The First Watch (6 p.m.-9 p.m.) J. E. Charles

everything about your life is spiritual, and you must see it from this perspective. Until you come to terms with this, you will sit around, fold your arms, and wait for good things to happen to you, which will only lead to defeat. Rather, you must learn to prayerfully engage each moment of the day and *decide* what happens to you. Know that as a child of God, you have a position of victory in Christ Jesus. However, as the Apostle Paul said in Ephesians 6, you need to be strong in the Lord and in the power of his *might,* and be fully equipped with the armor of God to stand against the wiles of the enemy.

You can only stand against the wiles of the enemy by tapping into God's power through *prayers.* And you have to be intentional and strategic about your prayers, keeping your spiritual antenna sensitive to the times and periods when the devil is set to embark on his mission.

God, through the Jewish calendar, divided the night and day into a series of *watches,* eight three-hour periods (four at night and four in the day), in which he desires his children to be *watchful for enemy activity,* just as the Old Testament guards stood watch on their towers to protect the city.

The first watch of the Jewish day started at sunset at 6 p.m. and lasted until 9 p.m. Today, our notion is that the new day starts at daybreak in the morning, but Israel considered the new day to start in the evening, according to the pattern God established in the creation:

And the evening and the morning were the first day. (Genesis 1:5)

So in the spirit realm when we talk of the *new day,* we mean sunset, and it is the time of the first watch, 6 p.m. to 9 p.m. Lamentations 2:19 tells us what is called for during this watch:

> *Arise, cry out in the night:* ***in the beginning of the watches pour out thine heart*** *like water before the face of the Lord:* ***lift up thy hands toward him*** *for the life of thy young children, that faint for hunger in the top of every street.*

The first watch is a time to *pour out thine heart* and *lift up thy hands* to the Lord—a time of prayer. At the end of a hectic day of work and errands, you may not feel like praying, but just kicking back and watching TV, but you need to understand that this is a key time to be alert for the devil's activity. You may be sure that he is not kicking back and relaxing when it comes to his attacks on you, your family, your church, and your nation, but is actively at work:

> *Be sober, be vigilant; because your adversary the devil walks about, seeking whom he may devour.* (1 Peter 5:8)

The First Watch (6 p.m.-9 p.m.) J. E. Charles

This first night watch is the pivotal time to "possess the gates"—that is, the *points of entrance*. There is a gate of entrance to every time, be it a new day or week or month or year. The first watch is the point of entry for the new spiritual day. It is the time to "possess the gates," which in ancient times meant to have control over your enemy. To "possess your gates" is to have power and authority of the devil, to lock him and his work out of your life. The best time to do this is at the start of the new spiritual day, the first night watch from 6 p.m. to 9 p.m.

When you are on your watchtower of prayer, you have authority over the enemy:

> *"Behold, I give unto you power to tread on serpents and scorpions, and over all the power of the enemy: and nothing shall by any means hurt you."* (Luke 10:19)

He will not be able to enter your gate.

Jesus modeled prayer for us in in the first night watch. In Matthew 14:15-22 we read that *As evening approached* (NIV) Jesus performed the miracle of the Feeding of the Five Thousand with the five loaves and two fish. Then Matthew 14:23-24 says:

> ***Immediately Jesus*** *made the disciples get into the boat and go on ahead of him to the other side, while he dismissed the crowd. After he had dismissed them, he*

went up on a mountainside by himself to pray. (Matthew 14:23-24, NIV, emphasis added)

After his day, Jesus *immediately* went to pray, modeling prayer for us in the first night watch. If Jesus needed this prayer time, how much more so do you and I!

Here are some mysteries of the first watch:

1. **It's the Time for Reflection and Meditation.** This is the watch when we reflect on our activities during the just-completed day—our decisions, relationships, words, and so on. We should also meditate on the Word of God—his promises concerning our lives, as Psalm 119:148 (NIV) says: *My eyes stay open through the watches of the night, that I may meditate on your promises.* By meditating on the Word of God, you free your spirit to be aligned with God to do his will and you also free your emotions by receiving peace from the Word.

2. **It's the Time for Healing.** The Bible records that Jesus Christ did some of his healing during this watch. This is seen in Mark 1:32 (NIV), which says, *That evening after sunset the people brought to Jesus all the sick and demon-possessed.* If God has given you the healing anointing, you should take this watch especially seriously.

3. **It's the Time for Covenant Renewal.** I mentioned that this period is the time to reflect. As you do so, it is important to rededicate yourself to God, renewing your covenant with him. The Apostle Paul wrote: *I protest by your rejoicing which I have in Christ Jesus our Lord,* ***I die daily*** (1 Corinthians 15:31, emphasis added). Dying daily means renewing our covenant to serve God every day. And it's best done during the first night watch.

4. **It's the Time to Receive Clear Directions for the Next Day.** You may have prepared your to-do list for the following day, but if God isn't there to guide you, you're one misstep away from failure. So get your to-do list from God, and be sensitive to his directions throughout the day. That will keep you from running around in circles.

5. **It's the Time to Pray for Your Children.** Notice the emphasis on praying for children in our Lamentations 2:19 text: *Arise, cry out in the night: in the beginning of the watches pour out thine heart like water before the face of the Lord: lift up thy hands toward him* ***for the life of thy young children****, that faint for hunger in the top of every street.* You must understand that the devil is out to attack your children, to make them useless, wayward, or worse. So in the first watch of the night pray for them, and declare judgment over

the enemy and his agents. In addition, claim the promises of God concerning your life and your family.

Prayers

- Every counterfeit cord, every ley line drawn against my dwelling, drawn against my properties, drawn against my body, drawn against my soul, drawn against my spirit line—with the Bible in my hand serving as a sword, I cut and burn the silver cord, I cut and burn the ley line.
- Every witchcraft-sponsored infirmity, *backfire* in Jesus's Name.

THE SECOND WATCH (9 P.M.-NOON)

At midnight I will rise to give thanks unto thee because of thy righteous judgments.

Psalm 119:62

The hour of *"midnight"* (the hour toward which the second watch leads) is also known as the *witching hour*, because it is the hour when the forces of darkness set in motion their plans. It is the hour when darkness is at its peak, and our sleep becomes most appealing to us. You're tucked in your duvet, covered with the cool frost of the air conditioner, and you feel like the sleep should last forever, because it feels good. However, in the realm of the spirit, it is the time when the enemy begins to bring to display his evil and diabolical plans. So for a child of God, this is not the time to sleep, but the time to rise up and revoke the arrows of the devil and seek God's protection.

One of the significances of the second prayer watch (leading up to midnight) is that it is the time when God releases judgments on the adversary and delivers his people from the bondage of the devil. But remember that God will not take action unless you engage with him in prayer. The Bible says, *The heaven, even the heavens, are the Lord's: but the earth hath he given to the children of men* (Psalm 115:16). God gave this realm to man, and he's never taken it back. He will wait until a human being invites him to work here through prayer, and then he will move, especially during this second watch of the night.

This is a strategic time to employ the whole armor of God, and abolish every demonic plan for your life, your family, the body of Christ, and the society at large. Yes, the coming midnight is the darkest hour, but you as a believer can always penetrate this darkness with prayer. God's light will drive out any darkness. Through prayer, and only through prayer, you can access places that may have seemed inaccessible to you, impenetrable.

Engaging in this second prayer watch, from 9 p.m. until the midnight hour, can bring clarity concerning the will of God for your life. And, beyond knowing what God wants you to do, you will be filled with the strength to fulfill your divine mission on earth. We see this modeled in the life of our Lord and Savior Jesus Christ in the Garden of Gethsemane:

Then cometh Jesus with them unto a place called Gethsemane, and saith unto the disciples, Sit ye here, while I go and pray yonder. And he took with him Peter and the two sons of Zebedee, and began to be sorrowful and very heavy. Then saith he unto them, my soul is exceeding sorrowful, even unto death: tarry ye here, and watch with me. And he went a little further, and fell on his face, and prayed, saying, O my Father, if it be possible, let this cup pass from me: nevertheless not as I will, but as thou wilt. (Matthew 26:36-39)

Bible historians tell us that Jesus went to Gethsemane to pray at the critical time of 9 p.m. Then, at about 11 p.m., he went back to check on his disciples and realized they were sleeping. It is also believed that Jesus came back the third time to his disciples by midnight—all during the second watch of the night. This was the most critical time in our Savior's life, and it seems that he was struggling to endure, as though his human nature had come to the end of its resources. The task appeared difficult and intense, and thus he expressed his natural human desire to avoid pain and suffering. Nonetheless, God sent him strength. How? Luke 22:43 says, *And there appeared an angel unto him from heaven, strengthening him.*

The same promise of divine strength and

encouragement applies to every believer who harnesses the power of the second night watch. God is waiting for you and me to try him and see if he will not do what he promised. Now there are more mysteries concerning the night watches, and I'll be sharing them below. So stick around and get ready to act in these critical hours.

1. **It's a Time for Divine Judgment and Deliverance**. The plans of the evil one are always set in motion in this watch, particularly as midnight approaches. So as God's children, we shouldn't sleep while the enemy is up and active, looking for how to destroy us. It's time for you and me to pray that God will scatter the encampment of the enemy, as David prayed in Psalms 68:1: *"Let God arise, let his enemies be scattered."*

    This is when we intercede for God's judgment on the evil ones and ask for deliverance upon our lives, and upon our loved ones. So keep watch at this time to break down the evil structures, assignments and systems set against you.

    The Scripture talks about the liberation of the Israelites from bondage in Exodus 11. They secured victory and matched out enriched at the second watch. This means that that this time is a very fiery time before God to bring judgment to all that has held you bound for years. And when

God delivers you from the enemy, he takes you to your land of inheritance and plenty!

2. **It's the Time for Divine Visitation.** Have you ever awakened from sleep and felt like something spectacular had happened to you at night? God loves to visit his children at night, or send his angels to do so. Just like in the case of Jesus in the Garden of Gethsemane, after he had prayed asking God to let the cup pass from him, yet still seeking that God's will be done: God sent his angel to minister strength to him. And there are other stories of people in the Bible who had encounters with God at night.

Prayers

- Every bondage of infirmities, *break* in Jesus's Name!
- Every curse of infirmities, *break* in Jesus's Name!
- Any man or woman that is visiting the grave for my sake, *die!* in Jesus's Name!

THE THIRD WATCH (MIDNIGHT-3 A.M.)

And at midnight Paul and Silas prayed, and sang praises unto God: and the prisoners heard them. And suddenly there was a great earthquake, so that the foundations of the prison were shaken: and immediately all the doors were opened, and every one's bands were loosed.

Acts 16:25-26

The third watch is one of the most sensitive watches, because it is a time filled with many spiritual activities, including that of demons. It is the watch when witches, necromancers, Satan, and his agents are busy carrying out their agenda. In this watch, they recite their incantations and summonses. Regrettably, this coincides with the deepest phase of human sleep, when you are completely unaware and ignorant of your environment. And Matthew 13:25 reveals what the enemy does when men sleep: *"But while men slept, his enemy came and sowed tares among the wheat, and went his way."*

The *"tares"* mentioned in that verse symbolize the works of havoc and destruction that the enemy inflicts upon humanity. It is imperative, therefore, that you be spiritually sensitive at this hour so that the adversary doesn't catch you off guard. Rather, you should take offensive action. Acts 16:25-26 reveals the power of midnight prayer:

> *And **at midnight Paul and Silas prayed, and sang praises** unto God: and the prisoners heard them. And suddenly there was a great earthquake, so that the foundations of the prison were shaken: and immediately all the doors were opened, **and every one's bands were loosed**.* (Emphasis added)

Paul and Silas understood the mystery behind midnight prayer, and they engaged in it accordingly. They didn't just pray, they sang. This means they were not quiet; they did not say, "Oh no, my neighbors might hear me." Men were all around them in the same jail as they sang and prayed. This was rugged prayer and praise. They could have just sat there and felt sorry for themselves, wallowing in self-pity. But they had revelation of what God can do in the midnight hour! And so they prayed and praised with gusto. I can hear them crying out and saying, "O Lord, please deliver us! Do not let the enemy mock at us. Show yourself strong on behalf of your servants."

Beloved, you can do the same. What is the situation that has you in chains, that has you locked up with no apparent way out? Can you learn from Paul and Silas? They knew that only God could save them from the adversary, and so they prayed and praised. And what was the result? *And suddenly there was a great earthquake, so that the foundations of the prison were shaken: and immediately all the doors were opened, and every one's bands were loosed.* The result was freedom! Not only for them, but for those around them. Are things dark? Is it midnight? Pray and praise, and experience God Almighty's deliverance!

Sometimes I wonder, What if they hadn't prayed? What if they had waited and assumed God would move on his own, because they were his servants? What if they had slept past the midnight hour? I doubt they would have received the same miracle.

The book of Acts contains the opposite example as well, the story of a young man who fell asleep in the midnight hour rather than engage in the spiritual:

> *And upon the first day of the week, when the disciples came together to break bread, Paul preached unto them, ready to depart on the morrow; and continued his speech until **midnight**. And there were many*

lights in the upper chamber, where they were gathered together. And there sat in a window a certain young man named **Eutychus, being fallen into a deep sleep**: *and as Paul was long preaching, he sunk down with sleep, and* **fell down from the third loft, and was taken up dead**. *And Paul went down, and fell on him, and embracing him said, Trouble not yourselves; for his life is in him.* (Acts 20:7-10)

Eutychus fell asleep on the watch and almost paid for it with his life. Because the devil is roaming about like a hungry lion looking for someone to devour, he goes for the believer who is spiritually weak, who is in a spiritual slumber, and he attacks. The slumber to which Eutychus succumbed did not look violent or dangerous, but he still fell. Are you still lost in spiritual sleep? It's time to wake up and face the enemy. Now consider these mysteries of the midnight watch:

1. **It's the Time for Warfare.** If you have been sleeping all your life, this is the time to wake up from that sleep. You must fight the devil and stop him from taking what God has ordained for you.
2. **It's the Time to Fix the Day Before It Starts.** By waging war at the midnight hour you can determine the next day's outcome before it begins,

solve the problems before they happen. It's the time to declare the roads accident-free as you go to and from work the next day, and to declare God's blessings on the other activities of the day.

PRAYERS

- Opportunity wasters, my life is not a candidate for your evil work, perish by fire in the name of Jesus.
- Spiritual chains binding my finances and progress, perish by fire in the name of Jesus.
- Spiritual powerlessness, perish by fire in the name of Jesus.

THE FOURTH WATCH (3 A.M.-6 A.M.)

*I remember thee upon my bed, and meditate
on thee in the night watches.*

Psalm 63:6

We come now to the fourth and final of the night watches, the watch that deals with the pre-dawn hours. A lot of battles are fought during this period. Research has shown that Roman battles were often waged between midnight and the early hours of the morning. This was one strategy that made Rome the great world power of their day, that enabled its soldiers to defeat the enemy: attacking when their foes were asleep. Hunters are also known to seek their game in the early morning hours when animals are less vigilant or even still asleep.

Likewise, the spiritual enemies of Christians like to

attack at night. That is why keeping watch at all times is necessary. No time is safe for the believer to fall asleep spiritually.

Peter is a good example of the danger of spiritual attack at night. It was in the hours of darkness that he denied the Lord three times, and specifically during this fourth watch of the night, just before the rooster crowed (John 18:27). The demons are in full force with spiritual activities during this time because men are asleep and not keeping watch to oppose them. They are therefore at liberty to release attacks, cast spells, and chant incantations without obstruction—thus the term *witching hour*.

As a child of God, you need to keep watch at this time to do spiritual battle. Do not be afraid, for God has given you all the authority to overcome them, as Jesus said:

> *"Behold, I give unto you power to tread on serpents and scorpions, and over all the power of the enemy: and nothing shall by any means hurt you."* (Luke 10:19)

Here are the mysteries of this watch hour:

1. **It is a Time to Hear God's Voice**. This is when God instructs his children. More so, he communicates his heart to us and reveals what the morning holds. However, unless you wake up and intercede, you won't hear him speaking to you. Samuel said, *"Here am I; for thou calledst*

me" (1 Samuel 3:5). Samuel wouldn't have heard the voice of the Lord if he wasn't sensitive in the night hour. Are you still caught up in slumber? It's time to arise and pray! As you engage with God, open your heart, and say, "Speak to me, Lord, I am ready to obey."

2. **It is a Time to Show Gratitude.** The first thing you ought to do when you wake from sleep is show gratitude to God for preserving your life. The Psalmist says, *Enter into his gates with thanksgiving, and into his courts with praise: be thankful unto him, and bless his name"* (Psalm 100:4). Your degree of gratefulness will determine how quickly you will access the throne of grace. Thanksgiving moves God to attend to us when we go to him in prayer. So you must learn the art of worship if you want to fully enter into the heart of God.

3. **It is the Time When the Heavenly and Earthly Realms Kiss.** At 3 a.m., the heavenly realm and earth come in contact. That is why the Almighty Elohim can come down to visit man at this time. The earth was made for man to inhabit, and it is dust; so the eternal spirits (angels and demons) don't reside here. However, at this time they are very strong on earth. Research has shown that the human body gets weak at 3 a.m., which is why much tragedy occurs at this hour. Therefore, it is

expedient to wake up and acquire mercy from God. The Scripture says, *Let us therefore come boldly unto the throne of grace, that we may obtain mercy, and find grace to help in time of need* (Hebrews 4:16).

4. **It is the Time When the Veil between the Heavenly and Earthly Realms is Thin.** This is when the spiritual realm tries to communicate with you. Now the spirit beings that attempt to come in contact with you are both the good and evil ones. You need to understand that it's not only Christians that can pray at 3 a.m. Spiritually evil people can also pray. Some people use this time to partner with the devil to commit havoc. You must get up and ask God to help you before the enemy ruins your life. You must tap into the anointing of the force of God at this time because he usually comes to earth at this time, just as the enemy does. Don't let the devil overcome you; stand up against him in victory by waking up to pray.

5. **It is the Time When Light and Darkness Marry.** The point where light and darkness meet is called "the force of creation," meaning "the force of Elohim." That is why you can create anything you want at this hour. Also, it is believed that the land of the living and the land of the dead are in contact at this hour. The earlier you engage with the throne of grace in prayer, the earlier you

will receive the needed help to fight against the kingdom of darkness.

6. **It is the Time for Renewal.** Dreams are one of the mediums God uses to reveal things to his people. It is wise to ask God for the grace to be attentive to the dreams he gives to you, or you will miss vital information that may affect your future. Also, God reveals the evil plans of the enemy through this means. When this happens, wake up and wage war before he gains an advantage over your life. As a Christian, it is crucial to live your life on vigil. There are levels you can never attain in the spirit without mastering the act of praying at night, as well as gates you can never access. There are deep revelations you will lose if you don't last on your knees at night. And, very importantly, there are Satanic alters, thrones, and chains that you can never dismantle except through rugged night prayers.

7. **It is the Time to Claim Your Blessing.** Jacob wrestled with the angel and secured his blessing during the fourth watch. *And he [the angel] said, Let me go, **for the day breaketh.** And he [Jacob] said, I will not let thee, except thou bless me* (Genesis 32:26, emphasis added). Jacob was persistent, wrestling with the angel all night until just as day was breaking—that is, at the end of the fourth watch—he received his blessing. You

likewise need to be persistent, reminding God of his promises and claiming them in your life. This is the time to do it.

8. **The News of the Birth of Our Lord Jesus Christ to the Shepherds.**

> *And there were shepherds in the same country abiding in the field, and **keeping watch by night over their flock. And an angel of the Lord stood by them**, and the glory of the Lord shone round about them: and they were sore afraid. And the angel said unto them, be not afraid; for behold, I bring you good tidings of great joy which shall be to all the people: for there is born to you this day in the city of David a Savior, who is Christ the Lord.* (Luke 2:8-11, emphasis added)

What if the shepherds had been asleep at this time? What if they had not been alert? I'm sure they wouldn't have received the good news. Can you now see why keeping watch is important? If we are not sensitive to the things of the spirit, we may miss the good news God has for us about ourselves, our family, and the body of Christ at large.

PRAYERS

- May my inner-man receive fire!
- By the power that healed blind Bartimaeus, O God, arise, heal me by fire!
- Every power of infirmity, be destroyed by fire in Jesus's Name.
- O the Immaculate, Omnipotent power of the blood of the Lamb, sanitize my blood!
- Every witchcraft-sponsored infirmity, *backfire* in Jesus's Name.

8

COMMAND THE MORNING

Very early in the morning, while it was still dark,
Jesus got up, left the house and went off to a solitary place,
where he prayed.

Mark 1:35, emphasis added

That transitional hour between the night and morning, the 3 a.m.-6 a.m. watch, sets the tone for the following day. Jesus knew this. That is why he arose *while it was still dark* to go and pray. Notice, it doesn't say he got up early to get an extra cup of coffee or catch the morning news or to have a few extra minutes to do his hair! He got up to pray.

The reason Jesus prepared for the new day with prayer, and the reason he wants us to do the same, is so that we won't be at the mercy of unforeseen circumstances and happenings. Rather, we can *command* our morning. That is, in the authority of Jesus' name and through the power of his Word, we can exercise dominion over that part of creation with which we have to do, according to God's original command to mankind:

> *And God blessed them, and God said unto them, Be fruitful, and multiply, and replenish the earth, and subdue it:* ***and have dominion*** *over the fish of the sea, and over the fowl of the air, and over every living thing that moveth upon the earth.*
> (Genesis 1:28, emphasis added)

WATCH!

This is the time for a disciplined prayer watch. Jesus said, *"But know this, that if the goodman of the house had known in what watch the thief would come, he would have watched, and would not have suffered his house to be broken up"* (Matthew 24:43). This is the time for those who have the power and training to wake up early and set the atmosphere for the coming day. This is the time to ensure that all of the enemy's plans and strategies for day will fail. This is the time to gain territory, establish the spirit of prosperity, and stop the devil from hijacking your blessings and favor. This prayer watch commands your day before it begins. This is an opportunity to set things in place before the devil and his demons have a chance to ruin them. Accidents, deaths, thefts, job losses, and all other acts of the devil can be stopped during this watch *when intercessors obey the voice of the Lord and fill the morning with powerful prayer.*

As you pray and declare God's Word, you will be releasing angelic activity:

> *Bless the Lord, ye **his angels**, that excel in strength, that do his commandments, **hearkening unto the voice of his word**.* (Psalm 103:20, emphasis added)
>
> *Are not all angels ministering spirits sent to serve those who will inherit salvation?* (Hebrews 1:14, NIV)

Heaven will intervene on your behalf!

STRIKE FIRST

Beloved, God does not want you to be a victim of your circumstances and of the attacks that this fallen world and the devil bring your way. Rather, he expects you to exercise dominion over spirits, men, and forces of nature. To do this, you must use the spiritual forces at your command, which are much more formidable than anything the devil can bring to the fight:

> *For the weapons of our warfare are not carnal, but mighty through God to the pulling down of strong holds.* (2 Corinthians 10:4)

Those *strongholds* include the *principalities, powers,* and *rulers of the darkness of this world,* and *spiritual wickedness in high places* (Ephesians 6:12). God has given you authority and dominion over the works of Satan's hands. In fact, he has put all things under your feet in Jesus (Ephesians 1:22; Psalm 8:3-6), which includes the sun, moon, and stars. Therefore, we are called to command our mornings and shake the wickedness out of our day (Job 38:12-13). You don't have to sit around and wait for the devil to act against you; you can *strike first* each morning and start the day with the upper hand.

COMMAND YOUR MORNING

In this chapter I will guide you in praying targeted prayers to strike first and cast the enemy out. Are you ready to command your morning? Then pray and declare with me:

Father, in Jesus' name...

- You have gone before me to prepare my way, to make the crooked way straight, and to make the rough way smooth. Father, I entrust my work to you, and you cause my plans to succeed, and everything I set my hands to do prospers (Proverbs 16:3). Father, today I have favor with all who look upon me and your favor surrounds me, enclosing me and covering me like a shield. You will work out your plans for my life because your faithful love endures forever.

- I declare and enforce your plans and purpose for my life over and against the plans and purpose of Satan. Satan, the blood of Jesus is against you. You have no authority over my life. No weapon that is used against me will succeed, and anyone who speaks against me will be proven wrong because my vindication comes from God (Isaiah 54:17).
- You will defeat my enemies; they will come against me but scatter before me in seven directions! (Deuteronomy 28:7)

Early Riser "I Am" Affirmations

1. I am a child of the King, an heir of God, and a joint heir with Christ.
2. I am more than a conqueror through him who loves me.
3. Fear has no place in my life because God has not given me a spirit of fear.
4. I am confident that no weapons formed against me will prosper, because God is for me—who can be against me?

5. Every curse spoken against me is to no avail because I am blessed.
6. Satan cannot curse those whom God has blessed.
7. I am blessed coming in and blessed going out.
8. My enemies shall come up against me one way, and God will cause them to flee in seven ways.
9. All that I set my hands to do will prosper.
10. All the people of the earth shall see that I am called by the name of the Lord.
11. The Lord has made me plenteous in goods.
12. I am a lender and not a borrower.
13. I am the head and not the tail.
14. I am above only and not beneath.
15. I am persuaded that neither death, nor life, nor angels, nor principalities, nor powers, nor things present, nor things to come, nor height, nor depth, nor any other creature shall be able to separate me from the love of God.

Amen.

SCRIPTURE CONFESSIONS

Psalm 5:1-3:

> *Give ear to my words, O Lord, consider my meditation. Hearken unto the voice of my cry, my King, and my God: for unto*

> *thee will I pray. My voice shalt thou hear in the morning, O Lord; in the morning will I direct my prayer unto thee, and will look up.*

Psalm 2:1-12:

> *Why do the heathen rage and the people imagine a vain thing? The kings of the earth set themselves, and the rulers take counsel together, against the Lord, and against his anointed, saying, Let us break their bands asunder, and cast away their cords from us. He that sitteth in the heavens shall laugh: the Lord shall have them in derision.*

> *Then shall he speak unto them in his wrath, and vex them in his sore displeasure. Yet have I set my king upon my holy hill of Zion. I will declare the decree: the Lord hath said unto me, Thou art my Son; this day have I begotten thee. Ask of me, and I shall give thee the heathen for thine inheritance, and the uttermost parts of the earth for thy possession. Thou shalt break them with a rod of iron; thou shalt dash them in pieces like a potter's vessel.*

Be wise now therefore, O ye kings: be instructed, ye judges of the earth. Serve the Lord with fear, and rejoice with trembling. Kiss the Son, lest he be angry, and ye perish from the way, when his wrath is kindled but a little. Blessed are all they that put their trust in him.

Psalm 121:1-8:

I will lift up mine eyes unto the hills, from whence cometh my help. My help cometh from the Lord, which made heaven and earth. He will not suffer my foot to be moved: he that keepeth me will not slumber. Behold, he that keepeth Israel shall neither slumber nor sleep. The Lord is my keeper: the Lord is my shade upon my right hand. The sun shall not smite me by day, nor the moon by night. The Lord shall preserve me from all evil: he shall preserve my soul. The Lord shall preserve my going out and my coming in from this time forth, and even for evermore.

Psalm 91:1-16:

He that dwelleth in the secret place of the most High shall abide under the shadow of the Almighty. I will say of the Lord, He is my refuge and my fortress: my God; in him will I trust.

Surely he shall deliver thee from the snare of the fowler, and from the noisome pestilence. He shall cover me with his feathers, and under his wings shalt I trust: his truth shall be my shield and buckler. I shalt not be afraid for the terror by night; nor for the arrow that flieth by day; Nor for the pestilence that walketh in darkness; nor for the destruction that wasteth at noonday.

A thousand shall fall at my side, and ten thousand at my right hand; but it shall not come nigh me. Only with my eyes shalt I behold and see the reward of the wicked. Because I have made the Lord, which is my refuge, even the most High, my habitation; There shall no evil befall me, neither shall any plague come nigh my dwelling. For he shall give his angels charge over me, to keep me in all my ways. They shall bear me up in their hands, lest I dash my foot against a stone. I shalt tread upon the lion and adder: the young lion and the dragon shalt I trample under feet. Because he hath set his love upon me, therefore will He deliver me: He will set me on high, because I have known His name. I shall call upon him, and He will answer me: He will be with me in trouble; He will deliver me, and honour me. With long life will He satisfy me, and shew me His salvation.

Psalm 16:1-11:

Preserve me, O God: for in thee do I put my trust. O my soul, thou hast said unto the Lord, Thou art my Lord: my goodness extendeth not to thee; But to the saints that are in the earth, and to the excellent, in whom is all my delight. Their sorrows shall be multiplied that hasten after another god: their drink offerings of blood will I not offer, nor take up their names into my lips.

The Lord is the portion of mine inheritance and of my cup: thou maintainest my lot. The lines are fallen unto me in pleasant places; yea, I have a goodly heritage. I will bless the Lord, who hath given me counsel: my reins also instruct me in the night seasons. I have set the Lord always before me: because he is at my right hand, I shall not be moved.

Therefore my heart is glad, and my glory rejoiceth: my flesh also shall rest in hope. For thou wilt not leave my soul in hell; neither wilt thou suffer thine Holy One to see corruption. Thou wilt shew me the path of life: in thy presence is fulness of joy; at thy right hand there are pleasures for evermore.

PRAYER POINTS

1. I take authority over this day, in the name of Jesus.
2. I draw upon heavenly resources today, in the name of Jesus.
3. I confess that this is the day that the Lord has made, I will rejoice and be glad in it, in the name of Jesus.
4. I decree that all the elements of this day will cooperate with me, in the name of Jesus.
5. I decree that these elemental forces will refuse to cooperate with my enemies this day, in the name of Jesus.
6. I speak unto you, O sun, moon, and stars; you will not smite me and my family this day, in the name of Jesus.
7. I pull down every negative energy planning to operate against my life this day, in the name of Jesus.

8. I dismantle any power that is uttering incantations to capture this day, in the name of Jesus.
9. I render null and void such incantations and satanic prayers over me and my family, in the name of Jesus.
10. I retrieve this day out of their hands, in the name of Jesus.
11. Let every battle in the heavenlies be won in favour of the angels conveying my blessings today, in the name Jesus.
12. O sun, moon, and stars, carry your afflictions back to your sender and release them against him, in the name of Jesus.
13. O God, arise and uproot everything that is working against me, in the name of Jesus.
14. Let the wicked be shaken out from the end of the earth, in the name of Jesus.
15. O sun, as you come forth, uproot all the wickedness that has come against my life, in the name of Jesus.
16. I program blessing unto the sun, the moon and the stars for my life today, in the name of Jesus.
17. O sun; cancel every daily evil program drawn against me, in the name of Jesus.
18. O sun, torment every enemy of the kingdom of God in my life, in the name of Jesus.
19. Those who spend the night pulling me down, O sun, throw them away, in the name of Jesus.

20. O elements, you shall not hurt me, in the name of Jesus.
21. O heavenlies, you shall not steal from my life today, in the name of Jesus.
22. I establish the power of God over the heavenlies, in the name of Jesus.
23. O sun, moon, and stars, fight against the stronghold of witchcraft targeted against me today, in the name of Jesus.
24. O heavenlies, torment every unrepentant enemy to submission, in the name of Jesus.
25. O heavens, fight against the stronghold of witchcraft, in the name of Jesus.
26. Every wicked altar in the heavenlies, I throw you down, in the name of Jesus.
27. Every cauldron in the star, moon, and sun, be broken, in the name of Jesus.
28. Every evil pattern in the heavenlies is broken, in the name of Jesus.
29. O God, arise and destroy every astral altar, in the name of Jesus.
30. I destroy every satanic connection between the heavenlies and my place of birth, in the name of Jesus.
31. Every spiritual wickedness in the heavenlies that will fight against me and my destiny today is disgraced by the blood of Jesus.

32. Thus saith the Lord, "Let no principality, power, ruler of darkness, spiritual wickedness trouble me, for I bear in my body the marks of the lamb of God." In the name of Jesus.
33. Every dark power hidden in the heavenlies against me, I pull you down in the name of Jesus.
34. Any evil power floating or hanging in the heavenlies against me, I bring you down, in the name of Jesus.
35. You the sun, moon, and stars, you shall favour me today, in the name of Jesus.
36. Every evil arrangement prepared by the sorcerers and witches against my life today, let them scatter and die, in the name of Jesus.
37. Any evil thing that will be programmed into the sun, the moon, and the stars against my life today, be dismantled, in the name of Jesus.
38. Every negative thing written in the cycle of the moon against me today is blotted out in the name of Jesus.
39. I shake off every season of frustration and failure, in the name of Jesus.
40. I dismantle every satanic calendar for my life today, in the name of Jesus.
41. Every evil word programmed against my star in the heavenlies shall not be established, in Jesus' name.

42. I terminate every evil agreement between my enemies and the heavenlies, in the name of Jesus.
43. Every evil handwriting programmed by satanic agents into the heavenlies against my life, be wiped out by the blood of Jesus.
44. I retrench and frustrate every satanic priest ministering enchantment into the sun, the moon, and the stars against my life, in Jesus' name.
45. I retrieve any of my properties dedicated to the sun, the moon, the stars, and the elements by the power of darkness, in Jesus' name.
46. You heavenlies, refuse to give a reply to any satanic programming against my life today, in Jesus' name.
47. Every wicked war working against me in the heavenlies, I overthrow you, in the name of Jesus.
48. (Point your finger to the sky as you make this prayer point.) Every negative thing programmed into the sun and the moon against my life today, be dismantled now, in Jesus' name.
49. Every power programming evil into my star, fall down and die, in the name of Jesus.
50. O Lord, cause my whole heart to be at rest, trusting in you today, in the name of Jesus.
51. O Lord, let my fellowship with you become greater today, in Jesus' name.
52. I stand against every satanic operation that would hinder my prayers today, in the name of Jesus.

53. Every wicked spirit planning to rob me of the will of God, fall down and die, in the name of Jesus.
54. I tear down the stronghold of Satan against my life, in the name of Jesus.
55. I bind every power cursing my destiny into ineffectiveness, in the name of Jesus.
56. I strike every evil power siphoning my blessing with chaos and confusion, in the name of Jesus.
57. I nullify the incantations of evil spiritual consultants, in Jesus' name.
58. I turn the evil devices of household witchcraft upside down, in Jesus' name.
59. I render every local satanic weapon harmless, in Jesus' name.
60. Every power cursing my destiny, be silenced, in the name of Jesus.
61. Today, I refuse to be in the right place at the wrong time, in Jesus' name.
62. I bind every negative energy in the air, water, and ground working against me, in the name of Jesus.
63. Anything from the kingdom of darkness that has made it their business to hinder me, I single you out right now and bind you, in the name of Jesus.
64. Be bound with chains that cannot be broken, in Jesus' name.
65. I strip off all your spiritual armor, in Jesus' name.
66. Lose the support of other evil powers, in the name of Jesus.

67. Do not involve yourself with me again, in Jesus' name.
68. Let the handwritings of ordinances programmed by satanic agents into the heavenlies against me be wiped out by the blood of Jesus.
69. I recover all my virtues dedicated to the elements in the name of Jesus.
70. You heavens and the elements, turn against every satanic programmer, in the name of Jesus.
71. Let the heavens declare the glory of God over my life, in the name of Jesus.
72. Everything programmed into my life in the heavenlies, I dismantle you, in the name of Jesus.
73. Spirit of favour, counsel, might, and power, come upon me, in the name of Jesus.
74. I shall excel this day and nothing shall defile me, in the name of Jesus.
75. I shall possess the gates of my enemies this day, in the name of Jesus.
76. The Lord shall anoint me with the oil of gladness above my fellows this day, in the name of Jesus.
77. The fire of the enemy will not burn me and my family this day, in the name of Jesus.
78. My ears shall hear good news and I shall not hear the voice of the enemy today, in the name of Jesus.
79. My life and the lives of the members of my family are secured in Christ, in the name of Jesus.

80. Let every satanic check point mounted against me in the heavenlies, be dismantled by the word of the Lord, in Jesus' name.

81. Every evil altar prepared against my breakthroughs in the heavenlies and in the sea, be dismantled by fire, in the name of Jesus.

82. You spiritual wickedness in the heavenlies militating against my star, I bring the hook of the Lord against you and frustrate your activities, in Jesus' name.

83. I receive open heavens for my life this day, in Jesus' name.

84. I take divine insurance against all forms of accident and tragedy, in the name of Jesus.

85. I send lightening, thunder, and the hook of the Lord against the evil queen in the heavenlies militating against me, in the name of Jesus.

86. Every evil spiritual equation programmed against my life, I command you to change, in Jesus' name.

87. I speak unto the headquarters of evil programmers and blow up their altars, in the name of Jesus.

88. Anything drawing power against me from the heavenlies, fall down and die, in the name of Jesus.

89. O Lord, give me the ability that is equal to my opportunity.

90. O Lord, empower me to pluck the seed of success, in Jesus' name.

91. O Lord, empower me to reach my goal, in Jesus' name.
92. O Lord, give me sufficient days to reach my goal, in the name of Jesus.
93. O Lord, guide my words and let them bear fruit, in Jesus' name.
94. O Lord, give me divine alertness to recognize divine opportunities.

Benediction

May the Lord Almighty hear the words of my confession today, for I declare them in the name of Jesus, who is *"the Apostle and High Priest of our profession"* (Hebrews 3:1), the mighty Savior-Warrior who goes forth to establish them on my behalf. *"Unto him that loved us, and washed us from our sins in his own blood, And hath made us kings and priests unto God and his Father; to him be glory and dominion for ever and ever. Amen."* (Revelation 1:5-6)

EARLY RISER CONFESSIONS FOR MINISTERS

Let the elders that rule well be counted worthy of double honour, especially they who labour in the word and doctrine.

1 Timothy 5:17

Just as *elders* (ministers) are to be considered *worthy of double honor* in the church, so are they to be held to higher standards of accountability. As Paul elsewhere counseled Timothy: *Take heed unto thyself, and unto the doctrine; continue in them: for in doing this thou shalt both save thyself, and them that hear thee* (1 Timothy 4:16).

So in this chapter I present to you, my fellow ministers, the following Early Riser Confessions and Intercessions to give you strength and encouragement as you lead God's church.

Prayers

Father, in the name of Jesus, I present my body to you as a living sacrifice, holy and acceptable as a reasonable service to you.

As a leader in the kingdom of God, I take seriously my charge to represent you, the kingdom, and your people at all times. I commit to live a lifestyle of holy fire that separates me from all unclean things. Lord, I thank you for giving me a clean heart and renewing in me a right spirit. Let a pathway be made in my heart and spirit that I may hear from you with clarity. Let my hearing be undefiled so that I may lead your people according to your will and your heart. Help me to discern your seasons and timing so that I may know your heartbeat. Let your kingdom come, and your will be done that the church may advance and follow the leading of the Holy Spirit.

Father prepare my heart and mind that I may not lean to my own understanding but will acknowledge you in all my ways. Give me a fresh anointing daily. As I put on the whole armor of God, I decree that no weapon will prosper against my family, my ministry, my city, my country, or me. Make known to me the deep revelations of the kingdom that I may become a repairer of the breach through warfare, intercession, and prayer. Equip me to destroy second-heaven activity and all the works of darkness.

The gates of hell will not prevail, for I am a godly

gatekeeper. I will guard the watches of the Lord and protect the sanctity of the vision of the Lord.

I commit to instruct your people in building walls of prayer. The enemy cannot penetrate, tear down, or destroy the prayer hedge of the Holy Spirit. I renounce the spirit of the "dog who has no bark." I will sound the alarm in Zion when trouble approaches. I pray that all leaders can come together and release one sound in the Spirit. I declare that there is no division, strife, envy, jealousy, contention, or hardness of heart among your spiritual eldership. We are fitly joined together and supplying every part needed for the perfecting of the saints. This unity of faith is releasing confusion in the enemy's camp. It is destroying every diabolical assignment, evil agenda, and wicked plan. The traps and snares intended for your sheep are uprooted by the prophetic anointing of Jeremiah.

Father, give me an eye in the Spirit that I may know how to navigate and maneuver in the things of the Spirit. Allow the smoke screen of the Holy Ghost to hide me from my enemies so that I can do the work of the Lord without bringing attention to myself. God, if you can use anything, use me! Thank you for allowing me to be a steward of the anointing. I renounce every spirit that would attempt to blind my mind to cause me to think that the great things I do are of me. I decrease so that the Holy Ghost may increase in my life. I am a servant of the Most High God, and I surrender all my allegiance to

Jesus. There is no room for compromise in my life. I love not my life unto death.

Out of my belly shall flow rivers of living waters. Declarations, decrees, and proclamations that flow from my lips shall he established in the life of every person, place, and thing they touch. I will stand in the righteousness of Christ because my righteousness is as filthy rags.

Lord, teach my hands to do war, for you are a God of war. In you there is no defeat. I claim every victory ahead of time. Jesus, you are my helper, and I thank you that I will not be deceived, pulled away, or caused to stray from the truth of your Word. The blood of Jesus protects and keeps me in all my ways so that my foot will not slip. And even if I fall, a righteous man will fall down seven times and get up every time.

Let the love of Christ shine from my soul so that men will be drawn to Jesus. Help me to love all people and show no partiality because of race, gender, financial status, political position, or appearance. I commit to serve your people and feed your sheep. Keep haughtiness, pride, and arrogance away from me. As I humble myself under your mighty hand, O God, you promised to exalt me in due season. Let all perversion, idolatry, covetousness, greed, and other sins of the priesthood be far away from me.

Idle words will not flow from my mouth by gossiping to cause scandal, shame, defamation of character, character assassination, or embarrassment, but my mouth will be filled with words to uplift and edify. I will know when and how to trouble Israel through correction and rebuke at the Lord's command, with no respect of persons or fear of man. I am a Zadok priest, and I will teach the people the difference between holiness and what is secular. I fear having a relationship with the people without having a relationship with God. My ministry is under an open heaven. Let the words of my mouth and the meditation of my heart be acceptable in your sight. Lord, you are my strength and my redeemer.

In Jesus' name, amen.

PART 3
UNRAVELING THE MYSTERIES OF THE DAY WATCHES

10

THE FIRST DAY WATCH (6 A.M.–9 A.M.)

*Cause me to hear thy loving kindness in the morning;
for in thee do I trust: cause me to know the way wherein
I should walk; for I lift up my soul unto thee.*

Psalm 143:8

Just as there are four night watches, there are four day watches, the first of which comes between 6 and 9 a.m. It is perhaps the most important of the day watches, for in it we start a new day—a new adventure in life.

The break of each new day is significant. Each morning signifies the start of something new: a new day, new passion, new vigor, new dreams and aspirations, and new hope for both that day and tomorrow. Each new day with God ushers in brilliant possibilities. And each new day can be the best you've ever had *if you begin it well*.

The First Day Watch (6 a.m.-9 a.m.) J. E. Charles

David reveals the way to start our day:

In the morning, Lord, you hear my voice; in the morning I lay my requests before you and wait expectantly. (Psalm 5:3, NIV)

David teaches that we should:

- Start our day with prayer— *In the morning, Lord, you hear my voice*
- Make our prayer requests of the Lord for that day— *in the morning I lay my requests before you*
- et out from that prayer time expecting and watching for the Lord's answers—*and wait expectantly*

Often, we're tempted to hit that snooze button and grab some extra sleep rather than get up in time to go before the Lord about our day, but how important it is to keep this first day watch prayerfully! As William law once said, *"The secret of a happy life is giving God the first part of your day, the first priority to every decision and the first place in your heart."*

How we spend the first part of our day reveals much about our esteem for the Lord, as David said in Psalm 63:1-2, *O God, thou art my God; early will I seek thee: my soul thirsteth for thee, my flesh longeth for thee in a dry and thirsty land, where no water is; to see thy power and thy glory, so as I have seen thee in the sanctuary.* We too can make this confession, if we will give the Lord the first part of our day in spite of our busy schedules, if we will be faithful to our morning *watch*.

A Mighty Outpouring

It was at the end of the first day watch, after the apostles had filled that watch with eager prayer, that the new era of the church—the era of the Holy Spirit—began.

> *And when the day of Pentecost was fully come, they were all with one accord in one place. And suddenly there came a sound from heaven as of a rushing mighty wind, and it filled all the house where they were sitting. And there appeared unto them cloven tongues like as of fire, and it sat upon each of them. And they were all filled with the Holy Ghost, and began to speak with other tongues, as the Spirit gave them utterance.* (Acts 2:1-4)

> *"For these are not drunken, as ye suppose, seeing it is **but the third hour of the day.**"* (Acts 2:15, emphasis added)

The *"third hour of the day"* was 9 a.m., the end of the first day watch. It was at this moment that the Holy Spirit began his last-day ministry in the world. As you tarry before him each morning, he will begin it anew each day through you.

When Herbert Jackson was assigned to the mission field, he was given a car that wouldn't start without a push. So he would round up kids from the school to give his car a push when he needed to go somewhere; or if he was out making his rounds, he'd either park on a hill or just leave the car running. He went through this trouble for two years.

When he was heading home, he was showing the new missionary what had to be done to get the car going. The new guy took a look under the hood, and said, "Uh, Dr. Jackson, I believe the only trouble is this loose cable." He gave the cable a twist, slid behind the wheel, and the engine roared to life. Dr Jackson later explained to a seminary class that for two years he'd pushed that car around, and all he needed to do was connect the cable.

As Christians, we often live in our own power, struggling and pushing to get by. But through our morning prayer we can "connect the cable" of our life to the Holy Spirit. We don't have to rely on our power alone. We can live in union with the omnipotent One.

ON HEALING WINGS

Another promise of the first day watch is healing:

> *But unto you that fear my name shall the Sun of righteousness arise with healing in his wings.* (Malachi 4:2)

Studies have shown that heart attacks are more severe in the morning.[1] If more people were starting the first watch of the day with the Holy Spirit, I believe we would see much less of this problem. The rising of the *Sun* would bring *healing in his wings*.

Prayers

- Every garment of darkness on my body, catch fire in the name of Jesus.
- O Lord, avenge my adversaries, before the breaking of the day, let them come to nothing.
- Powers of environmental covens, be destroyed by fire in the name of Jesus

---

[1] https://www.webmd.com/heart-disease/news/20110427/heart-attacks-in-the-morning-are-more-severe

THE SECOND DAY WATCH (9 A.M.–NOON)

What would a typical day be without work? In every race, tribe, and language, work is one of the activities that gives dignity and honor to everyone who engages in it. Steven C. Preston, CEO of Goodwill Industries International, said, "Work can help any private or public institution address some of the most intractable social issues we face with dynamic solutions." The second day watch spans the hours from 9 a.m. until noon, hours during which activities are generally at their peak, especially when it comes to work.

Jesus knew the importance of the daytime hours for work. He said in John 9:4, *"I must work the works of Him that sent me, while it is day, night cometh, when no man can work."* Jesus knew the importance of this morning watch and so set himself up to work in it. The fact is, a man who does not utilize this morning period for work will eventually find that he has nothing going for him at night or in the days to come. Genesis 49:27 says, *"In the morning he shall devour the prey,"* which taken metaphorically means we must do the hard work now so that in the days ahead we will be fruitful.

Jesus introduced one of his parables as follows:

> *"For the kingdom of heaven is like unto a man that is an householder, which went out early in the morning to hire labourers into his vineyard. And when he had agreed with the labourers for a penny a day, he sent them into his vineyard.* ***And he went out about the third hour, and saw others standing idle in the marketplace, And said unto them; Go ye also into the vineyard****, and whatsoever is right I will give you. And they went their way."* (Matthew 20:1-4, emphasis added)

Notice that the *"householder"* in this parable *"went out about the third hour"* to find, to his surprise, men *"standing idle"* and not working. The third hour was nine o'clock in the morning, the hour at which the second day watch begins. The second day watch is a time for work, not for *"standing idle in the marketplace."*

There are significant spiritual mysteries tied to the second day watch, which we'll look at now:

The Second Day Watch (9 a.m.-Noon)   J. E. Charles

HE WAS CRUCIFIED FOR OUR SAKE

Jesus was crucified for our salvation at the beginning of the second day watch:

> And when they had crucified him, they parted his garments, casting lots upon them, what every man should take. **And it was the third hour**, and they crucified him. And the superscription of his accusation was written over, THE KING OF THE JEWS." (Mark 15:24-26, emphasis added)

During this period of the day set aside for work, Jesus did the *ONE GREAT WORK* that bought our salvation, that made it unnecessary for us to have to work for our own salvation, a task we could never have accomplished. His death, followed by his glorious resurrection three days later, ushered in the Age of Grace. Not only did he take our sins, sicknesses, poverty, and judgement upon himself on the cross, but he demolished the wall that divided Jew from Gentile and, most importantly, the wall that divided us from union with our Heavenly Father. This hour, therefore, is an appropriate time to pray the benefits of the cross into reality in our lives and family. This is the time to thank and glorify God for the sacrifice he made on the cross of Calvary.

FORGIVE, AS YOU HAVE BEEN FORGIVEN

Not only should we celebrate our forgiveness by God in this watch, we should also extend that forgiveness to others. What God has freely given to us, we should give to others, as it is written:

> *And be ye kind one to another, tenderhearted, forgiving one another, even as God for Christ's sake hath forgiven you.* (Ephesians 4:32)

Are you finding it difficult to let go of hurt, bitterness, and anger? Do you know that withholding forgiveness can engender negative emotions within you that will distort your perception of life? Lewis B. Smedes once said, "To forgive is to set a prisoner free and discover that the prisoner was you." I understand how difficult it is to let go of some deep-seated hurts inflicted upon you, beloved, but keep in mind that the Lord suffered more. He was crucified for deeds he did not commit. Therefore, take advantage of this moment of the day to forgive and to ask God to heal your heart so that his love can fill it to overflowing.

INTERCESSION

This hour of the day should also inspire intercession in our lives, the act of praying for others. For on the cross, Jesus was bearing our griefs and sorrows, as Isaiah prophesied:

> *He is despised and rejected of men; a man of sorrows, and acquainted with grief: and we hid as it were our faces from him; he was despised, and we esteemed him not. Surely he hath borne our grief, and carried our sorrows.* (Isaiah 53:3-4).

Glory to God! As Jesus died to carry our griefs and sorrows away, let us pray at this hour for Christians who are sorrowful or in pain to be freed from their afflictions. Let us intercede for our brothers and sisters in Christ. And if you yourself are suffering, please remember that Jesus didn't bear that grief upon himself just so you could take it back; no, leave it with him, beloved—he is big enough to handle it.

DIVINE PROVISION

The second day watch is the time to pray for divine provision for your needs.

And the children of Israel did according to the word of Moses; and they borrowed of the Egyptians jewels of silver, and jewels of gold, and raiment: And the Lord gave the people favour in the sight of the Egyptians, so that they lent unto them such things as they required. And they spoiled the Egyptians.
(Exodus 12:35-36)

When God freed Israel from Egyptian slavery, he instructed Moses to tell the people to collect silver, gold, and other precious items from their Egyptian masters. Without hesitation, the Egyptians responded favorably to their requests and provided them with all sorts of goods.

You might wonder why there would be any need for something like gold since the Israelites were heading for the wilderness, but during the construction of the tabernacle in the wilderness gold, silver, linen, and other such materials were needed in order to construct God's dwelling among the Israelites. God, who knows the beginning from the end, was providing for Israel ahead of time.

You see, whatever God has planned for your future, he will be sure to provide for it. He will not let you get stranded along the way; he will be there for you with his supernatural supply.

Jesus demonstrated this truth when he sent his disciples out on a mission:

> *And He said to them, Take nothing for the journey, neither staffs or bag nor bread nor money; and do not have two tunics apiece. Whatever, house you enter, stay there, and from there depart. And whoever will not receive you, when you go out of that city, shake off the very dust from your feet as a testimony against them.* (Luke 9:3-5)

Interestingly, some time later (in Luke 22:35) Jesus made reference to this mission trip, and asked the disciples, *When I sent you without purse, and scrip, and shoes, lacked ye anything? And they said, Nothing.* He didn't ask the disciples how many people got saved or healed, but if they had lacked provisions for the journey. God takes his responsibility to provide for his servants seriously.

If you have been given a dream, purpose, or vision that is being impeded through lack of resources, now is the time, during this second day watch, to earnestly seek God for the supplies needed for your assignment. (Philippians 4:19)

PUT OFF THE OLD MAN

> *I am crucified with Christ: nevertheless I live; yet not I, but Christ liveth in me: and the life which I now live in the flesh I live by*

*the faith of the Son of God, who loved me,
and gave himself for me.* (Galatians 2:20)

The crucifixion, begun during this second watch of the day, means that we have been given new life in Christ, and that our old way of life must be done away with. We are no longer to be controlled by the dictates of the flesh, and tossed to and fro by fads and fancies, but now we can live and be influenced by the power of the Holy Spirit.

Therefore, during this watch, seek help to overcome the deeds of the flesh as listed in Galatians 5:19-21: *Adultery, fornication, uncleanness, lasciviousness, Idolatry, witchcraft, hatred, variance, emulations, wrath, strife, seditions, heresies, Envyings, murders, drunkenness, revellings, and such like.* Instead, determine to live by the power of the Holy Spirit.

The Bible says in Hebrews 4:15, *For we have not an high priest which cannot be touched with the feeling of our infirmities; but was in all points tempted like as we are, yet without sin.* God knows about the challenges you face each day and how much you desire to be like him. Therefore, pray for the power to live above sin so you can manifest the treasures embedded in the crucified life.

Counselling sessions are good, therapy is helpful, rehab is vital. However, lasting help is available only in Jesus Christ. Therefore, during this watch, pray for the power to stand against the wiles of the devil so you can freely spread the fragrance of Christ everywhere.

PRAYERS

- I overcome the devil by the power of the blood of the Lamb of the living God and the word of my testimony.
- I have been raised up to sit together with Christ by grace. By the power of resurrection, I have been raised up with Christ.
- Christ has raised me up from the death of sin and sorrow.

12

THE THIRD DAY WATCH (NOON-3 P.M.)

Noon marks the beginning of the third day watch, and that brightest part of the day in which the sun gives its optimum brightness to the world. Strangely enough, however, it was during this watch that the greatest darkness in the history of the world occurred, a supernatural darkness:

> Now from **the sixth hour** there was darkness over all the land unto **the ninth hour.** (Matthew 27:45, emphasis added)

Jesus was crucified at the beginning of the second day watch, at nine in the morning, but it was at the beginning of the third day watch, at noon (*the sixth hour*), when thick darkness fell over the earth, a darkness that lasted until 3 p.m. (*the ninth hour*). Why the darkness? This was the period during which the Father turned his face away from the Son as the Son bore our sin on the cross: Jesus was experiencing the punishment we deserved, including separation from his Heavenly Father, at that moment.

The third day watch, therefore, should remind us to pray for the deliverance of those who are still in darkness, to pray that the light of the gospel will shine into their heart:

> *But if our gospel be hid, it is hid to them that are lost: In whom the god of this world hath blinded the minds of them which believe not, lest the light of the glorious gospel of Christ, who is the image of God, should shine unto them.* (2 Corinthians 4:3-4)

Have you wondered why some individuals are so bent on sponsoring evil activities? It's because the devil has darkened their minds and only the light of the gospel can peel back the layers of darkness and reveal the truth.

This is what happened to Saul, the church's chief persecutor, to turn him into the Apostle Paul, the church's greatest champion. He was on his way to punish more of these new Christians for their faith when, as he himself described it to King Agrippa:

> *"Whereupon as I went to Damascus with authority and commission from the chief priests, At midday, O king, I saw in the way a light from heaven, above the brightness of*

the sun, shining round about me and them which journeyed with me." (Acts 26:12-13)

This reveals that the light of Christ shines even brighter than the sun, and there is no sinner, no matter how hardened, who cannot be enlightened by its unveiling. Do you have someone in your life who is stuck deep in the quagmire of sin? Are you on the verge of giving up because you have tried everything but the situation seems the same? Now, during the third day watch, raise prayers of intercession to God on their behalf. God has reserved this moment to shine his light and open their heart to the gospel of Christ.

Shine Forth, Shine Bright

Yes, Jesus is the brightest light, the light that dims the sun by comparison:

> *And he had in his right hand seven stars: and out of his mouth went a sharp twoedged sword: and his countenance was as the sun shineth in his strength.* (Revelation 1:16)

But he has not kept this light to himself:

> *For **God**, who commanded the light to shine out of darkness, **hath shined in our***

> ***hearts**, to give the light of the knowledge of the glory of God in the face of Jesus Christ.*
> (2 Corinthians 4:6, emphasis added)

He has given us the same light of Christ to shine *in* our lives and *through* our lives to others. Henceforth, beloved, see yourself as a light to your world. Now is the time to pray against factors that do not represent or glorify God in your life, family, business, career, or relationships. As nothing can stop the sun from rising to its peak and shining each day, nothing can stop you from rising and shining—from rising to the peak of his purpose and influence in your life.

That is why Proverbs 4:18 reads, *But the path of the just is as the shining light, that shineth more and more unto the perfect day.* Your path, as you follow God, is going to grow brighter and brighter by the day. Therefore, lay hold of God's promises and claim them in your life. Speak brightness into the dark places in your life. Declare the glory of God into areas that are not in harmony with God.

UNDER THE SHADOW OF GOD'S WINGS

> *He that dwelleth in **the secret place of the most High** shall abide under the shadow of the Almighty. I will say of the LORD, He is my refuge and my fortress: my God; in him will I trust. Surely he shall deliver*

> *thee from the snare of the fowler, and from the noisome pestilence. He shall cover thee with his feathers, and under his wings shalt thou trust: his truth shall be thy shield and buckler.* (Psalm 91:1-4, emphasis added)

There is no safer place on earth than the *secret place* of the Almighty. The secret place of the Most High is a place of *refuge* from the *snares* and *pestilences* of the enemy. And notice that the enemy's attacks occur in the daytime too:

> *Thou shalt not be afraid for the terror by night; nor for* **the arrow that flieth by day***; Nor for the pestilence that walketh in darkness; nor for* **the destruction that wasteth at noonday***.* (Psalm 91:5-6, emphasis added)

Just as the nighttime witnesses the attacks of the enemy, the psalmist tells us that the day can be filled with unseen battles too. Therefore, we need to stay in that *secret place* of God's protection, and yet at the same time be ready to rise up in prayer and combat the tragedies that the enemy seeks to visit upon individuals, families, and nations—the acts of *destruction that wasteth at noonday*.

During this watch, while you abide in the *secret place,* legislate your authority over the activities of the devil. Pray for God's protection over your family. Pray for divine protection over your resources, employees, ministerial staff, business, or partnerships.

Just as people seek shelter from the heat of the sun at this time of the day, likewise it's time to seek divine shelter from the heat of the devil. Heat signifies harshness, uneasiness, and inconvenience. This is the devil's strategy to make life uneasy and difficult for God's saint. But you have a *secret place* in which to abide, in the cooling *shadow of the Almighty.* Proverbs 18:10 declares: *The name of the LORD is a strong tower: the righteous runneth into it, and is safe.*" It is time to run to the abode of the Almighty, where no messenger from the pit of hell can reach.

Prayers

- I am desperate for healing, O Lord, like blind Bartimaeus. I am not ashamed, heal me, O Lord, heal my spouse, heal my children, heal my infirmity, heal my soul.
- Anywhere my name is called for evil, let my angel be instructed now to cut off their head in the Name of Jesus.
- Whatever spirit that is strengthening the stronghold of sin in me, let it be blotted out with the blood of Jesus.

13

THE FOURTH DAY WATCH (3 P.M.-6 P.M.)

With the fourth day watch, from three in the afternoon until six in the evening, we bring the cycle of the day to a close. The Jews considered the evening to be the start of the next new day, according to the pattern set by God at creation:

> *And the evening and the morning were the first day.* (Genesis 1:5)

So this fourth watch of the day signals completeness, that time of day when businesses are closing up shop and commuters are heading home and students are laying down their books. It is a time to take a deep breath, aware that the stress of the day has ended, to rest, and to reflect on how the day was spent.

Yet in this fourth day watch are some powerful mysteries to know and take spiritual advantage of. In fact, out of all the watches, it is the fourth day watch that is said to contain the *hour of prayer:*

> *Now Peter and John went up together into the temple at the **hour of prayer, being the ninth hour*** [i.e., 3 p.m.] (Acts 3:1, emphasis added).

Let's look at the mysteries associated with this watch.

A TIME FOR MIRACLES

The fourth day watch is the time for long-awaited miracles to occur:

> *¹ Now Peter and John went up together into the temple **at the hour of prayer, being the ninth hour.***
>
> *² And a certain man lame from his mother's womb was carried, whom they laid daily at the gate of the temple which is called Beautiful, to ask alms of them that entered into the temple;*
>
> *³ Who seeing Peter and John about to go into the temple asked an alms.*
>
> *⁴ And Peter, fastening his eyes upon him with John, said, Look on us.*

⁵ And he gave heed unto them, expecting to receive something of them.

⁶ Then Peter said, Silver and gold have I none; but such as I have give I thee: In the name of Jesus Christ of Nazareth rise up and walk.

⁷ And he took him by the right hand, and lifted him up: and immediately his feet and ankle bones received strength.

*And he leaping up stood, and walked, and entered with them into the temple, **walking, and leaping, and praising God**.*

⁹ And all the people saw him walking and praising God.

- Acts 3:1-7 (emphasis added)

This was one of the most notable miracles performed through the apostles in the early days of the church. This man had been lame from birth, with no chance to work for himself or have a normal life; instead, he had to sit outside the church begging—for there were no government welfare programs in those days. And he was forty years old, we learn from Acts 4:22. And now, after Peter and John prayed for him, he is *walking, and leaping, and praising God* for all the people to see!

For forty years, his condition defied human solutions, until Jesus came along inside his two disciples. This tells us that the fourth day watch is the time for long-awaited miracles. Are you a minister or a believer who longs to see people freed from the bondage of sickness and sorrow? This fourth day watch, at the hour of prayer, is the perfect time to press into God and see these miracles happen.

Assurance

It was at the beginning of the fourth day watch, at three in the afternoon, that the most significant words in history were uttered. Put the following Scripture texts together and you will find out what these words were:

> And **about the ninth hour** Jesus cried with a loud voice, saying, Eli, Eli, lama sabachthani? that is to say, My God, my God, why hast thou forsaken me? ... Jesus, when he had cried again with a loud voice, yielded up the ghost. (Matthew 27:46, 50, emphasis added)

> *When Jesus therefore had received the vinegar, he said,* ***It is finished****: and he bowed his head, and gave up the ghost.* (John 19:30, emphasis added).

The cosmos-shaking words that Jesus uttered at the beginning of the fourth day watch were *"It is finished."* He was declaring that the final and only sacrifice for sin had been made with his death on the cross, and salvation had been completely purchased for you and me—it had been *paid in full* (which is another way to translate his statement).

At this moment more than 300 prophecies in Scripture concerning the birth, life, ministry, and death of the Messiah were fulfilled. At this moment the history of mankind changed drastically. At this moment man, who had lost his heritage in the fall, found his way back to God. At this moment the veil in the temple was torn in two to signify that the way into God's presence had been opened (Matthew 27:51). At this moment we found new life in Christ. At this moment the works of the devil were over. IT IS FINISHED! *Paid in full!*

So at this time of the day, beloved, is the perfect time to remember that your salvation—your forgiveness, your healing, your prosperity, your eternal home in heaven—has been completely provided for you. The work is done. In fact, it's so done that the New Testament says that in the mind of God we are already seated with him in heaven:

> *And hath raised us up together, and made us sit together in heavenly places in Christ Jesus.* (Ephesians 2:6)

WHETHER JEWS OR GREEK

Perhaps you have had the queasy feeling at one point in your life of being excluded—passed over for the promotion, picked last for the team, rejected for the other suitor. Well, when it comes to God, *no one is excluded!* This is another truth emphasized in the fourth day watch, as we read in Scripture:

> *He saw in a vision evidently **about the ninth hour of the day** an angel of God coming in to him, and saying unto him, Cornelius.* (Acts 10:3)

Thus begins the account of salvation coming to the Gentiles, that is, to the non-Jewish world. Cornelius was a Roman centurion, into whose home a good Jew would never deign to enter. But through the instructions of this angel, who visited Cornelius at the beginning of the fourth day watch (*about the ninth hour of the day*, i.e., *the hour of prayer*), the Apostle Peter would come and share the Gospel with Cornelius and other Gentiles, and the door of faith was thrown wide open to the whole world—to you and me and everyone else. The Apostle Paul declared God's inclusiveness in these words:

> *There is neither Jew nor Greek, there is neither bond nor free, there is neither male nor female: for ye are all one in Christ Jesus.* (Galatians 3:28)

There are no color or racial or national or economic exclusions in God's family. All who put their faith in his Son are welcome:

> *For ye are all the children of God by faith in Christ Jesus.* (Galatians 3:26)

Beloved, you are accepted. Enjoy your fellowship with the Father!

Prayers

- My Father, I am in your courtroom, judge my adversaries, in the Name of Jesus!
- I drag domestic witchcraft to the court of the Almighty. Let God arise in the Name of Jesus and judge them by fire!
- I drag all my stubborn enemies to the court of Almighty. Let God arise in the Name of Jesus and judge them by fire!

PART 4
UNRAVELING THE MYSTERIES OF THE SEASONS OF POWER

14

SOLSTICE

To everything there is a season, and a time to every purpose under the heaven.

Ecclesiastes 3:1

Have you ever stepped outside to see the rising or setting of the sun? If you have, you have seen God's beautiful artistry on display, glorious spectacles that have inspired poets and lovers and painters for millennia. But there is another purpose for the circuit of the sun and the other celestial bodies on their courses through the heavens, and that is to give order and purpose to human life:

> *And God said,* ***Let there be lights in the firmament of the heaven*** *to divide the day from the night; and let them be **for signs**, and **for seasons**, and **for days**, and*

years*…*And God made two great lights; the greater light to rule the day, and the lesser light to rule the night: he made the stars also. (Genesis 1:14, 16, emphasis added)

The Bible says that God gave us the sun, moon, and stars to mark *days, seasons,* and *years* for us. In so doing, God gave a double blessing:

1. He provided variety. As much as we love the sunrise, would we enjoy it as much without first experiencing the night? As much as we glory in a summer's day, isn't it all the sweeter as we recall the winter's cold?
2. He provided order. The days and seasons and years give direction in life. We sleep at night, plant in the spring, and delight in grandchildren in our later years.

The sun is the chief of the heavenly lights. Its solstices—the two days each year when it is farthest north and south of the equator (Merriam Webster)—mark the beginnings of summer and winter, and its equinoxes—the two days each year when it crosses the plane of the equator—mark the beginnings of spring and fall.

In the following chapters we'll discuss the solstices and equinoxes that God has given us, which I refer to as *the seasons of power.* That is because there is a divine purpose for each of them, which we must live in harmony with in order to live wisely. In fact, if we don't recognize the purposes of the seasons, we will not live at all—that is, if we tried to plant in winter or forgot to harvest in fall, we would literally starve to death. That's how important it is to realize, as Solomon wrote, that *To everything there is a season.* (Ecclesiastes 3:1).

Likewise, there are different seasons in our personal lives, which also must be recognized and lived in harmony with in order to experience God's good plan for us. As we look at the different seasons of the year that God has ordained in the earth, we will also learn important lessons for living the seasons of our life to the full.

God in Control

But as we look at the seasons that develop as a result of the sun's circuit through the heavens, don't make the mistake that pagans made through the centuries, and that some even make today, and ascribe any divine qualities to the sun. It is a mere creation of our great Heavenly Father, who retains all authority and power over it.

Do you recall the story of Joshua from the Old Testament? How in order to fully defeat Israel's enemy it was necessary for the day to be prolonged? Impossible, right? Well, not with our God. The Bible says:

> ***And the sun stood still***, *and the moon stayed, until the people had avenged*

> *themselves upon their enemies. Is not this written in the book of Jasher?* **So the sun stood still in the midst of heaven, and hasted not to go down about a whole day.** (Joshua 10:13, emphasis added)

Can you imagine the incomparable power this miracle involved, arresting the very motions of the universe? It is mindboggling, but our God did it to bring his servants victory. If your seasons have gotten out of whack, beloved, fear not! God has control over the whole universe and time itself. He can put it all back together again.

The truth is, the Bible says he has given *you* authority over everything he created:

> *And God blessed them, and God said unto them, Be fruitful, and multiply, and replenish the earth, and subdue it: and* **have dominion** *over the fish of the sea, and over the fowl of the air, and over every living thing that moveth upon the earth."* (Genesis 1:28, emphasis added)

What that means is this: When you are on-mission with God, following his course for your life, your prayers have the power of Almighty God backing them. Even nature, including the times and seasons, must obey.

PRAYERS

- My Father, you are the one who created time and seasons, and you put me here to operate; so by the power of the *Holy Ghost,* I recover my destiny, my power, my health, my smile, my joy—I recover them back, in Jesus's Name.
- Any power prolonging infirmities in my life, *die* in Jesus's Name.

SUMMER SOLSTICE—A TIME FOR WORK

The ants are a people not strong, yet they prepare their meat in the summer.

Proverbs 30:25

Summer is the season of warmth and heat. It is associated in most people's minds with that time in life when everything is at its finest, the trees and plants in full bloom. It is the prime time of life. It is a time of activity. Summer represents a season to *gather* or *put together*. Summer provides an opportunity to work.

When is *your* summer? Remember, Solomon pointed out that there is a time for everything on earth. And remember, God created everything for a purpose. Your summer represents your season of plenty and abundance, your season of strength, your season of good weather.

It's important to recognize your time of opportunity.

In our text, the Bible points out that even ants know the proper time to go out and collect and prepare. Imagine if they tried to gather in the wrong season. They would go hungry during winter if they failed to gather in summer—they might go into extinction!

Likewise, you and I need to prepare in the summer seasons of our life. Are you taking advantage of the opportunities around you? Are you growing in knowledge, and utilizing the knowledge you already have? Are you growing in your skills, and utilizing those you already have? Take example from the ants, beloved!

God has attached destinies to your life, and what you do with the opportunities that come in your *summer* will determine whether you fulfill them or not, whether or not you'll be prepared for your *winter*. Jesus knew his mission on earth. He said through the psalmist: *"I delight to do thy will, O my God: yea, thy law is within my heart"* (Psalm 40:8). He knew that the fate of the whole world rested on his shoulders, and he made use of his summer to work and pray, and thus he succeeded. He *gathered* souls for the harvest (winter) time.

Summer is a time to sweat. Although God said, *"In the sweat of thy face shalt thou eat bread,"* (Genesis 3:19), yet he also said, *"the labour of the righteous tendeth to life"* (Proverbs 10:16). And he went further to promise the righteous: *"for thou shalt eat the labour of thine hands: happy shalt thou be, and it shall be well with thee"* (Psalm 128:2). The dignity of labor is enjoyed only in God. This means when you seek God and his will, your summertime will be a blessing.

Prayers

- I pray against every devil assigned to wage war against me and my family.
- I fire back every arrow of the serpent assigned against me, I cast and bind them out. I place in their jaw the hook of the living God; I place the hook of fire on them in the name of Jesus!

16

WINTER SOLSTICE— HARVEST TIME

As the cold of snow in the time of harvest, so is a faithful messenger to them that send him: for he refresheth the soul of his masters.

Proverbs 25:13

While summer represented a time of labor and preparation, winter represents a time of harvest (Proverbs 6:8; 10:5), a time to enjoy the fruit of our labor. Thus, winter is a picture of joy for those who have worked in summer but a picture of gloom and regret for those who failed to work. The truth is, everyone will harvest what they have used their opportunities for:

> *Be not deceived; God is not mocked: for whatsoever a man soweth, that shall he also reap.* (Galatians 6:7)

You may think little is required of you during winter, but in reality it is to be a time of reflection, inward-searching, self-evaluation. Winter is a time of cold, when there is less outdoor activity. God wants us to use that time for self-appraisal, to weigh whether we have used or abused our opportunities.

> *For if we would judge ourselves, we should not be judged.* (1 Corinthians 11:31)

A certain species of bears hibernates for six months during the winter. So during the summer they accumulate as much body fat as possible. The wintertime would not give them the opportunity to find food as summertime does. They make the most of their opportunity. Whether they will survive the winter depends on their summer.

Winter is a time to take stock of the year and compare your results to your expectations. Did you outperform your expectations? Did you underperform? Or were you right on point? Winter is a time to answer the question: How did I use my summer?

Winter, as a period of harvest, also provides an opportunity to help others. Ruth gleaned from Boaz's farm during harvest, providing a way for Boaz to help poor Naomi. But it also opened a door of blessing for Boaz. He got a godly wife in Ruth.

Prayers

- I claim the harvest of my *"well doing"* (Galatians 6:9) in my life, in Jesus' name.
- I thank God that, in accordance with his promise in Deuteronomy 28:11, he has made me *"plenteous in goods, in the fruit of [my] body, and in the fruit of [my] cattle, and in the fruit of [my] ground, in the land which the Lord sware"* to give to me.

EQUINOX—A BALANCED LIFE

In the day of prosperity be joyful, but in the day of adversity consider: God also hath set the one over against the other, to the end that man should find nothing after him.

Ecclesiastes 7:14

The equinoxes are the two days in the year when day and night are of equal length (the word equinox is derived from Latin words meaning *equal night*, and thus suggests as well an equal day). On the autumnal equinox and on the spring equinox there are equal hours of sunlight and darkness, which means equal opportunity. Irrespective of your location on earth, from the poles to the equator, and across the oceans to the deserts, equal opportunity abounds for all men. The equinox represents balance.

Life is all about finding balance. But you may ask,

"Why must I find balance?" Because life has ups and downs. Therefore, finding equilibrium is necessary for survival. Beyond this, it's the way God ordained life. The verse above talks about the days of prosperity and the days of adversity. You probably have unanswered questions about life, such as, "Why are some people seemingly better off and some are seemingly worse off?"

Consider the piano with black and white keys. Why are the keys not all white? White communicates absence of problems, and the presence of purity and calmness. But without the black keys, there cannot be harmony. The black keys complement the white keys to produce melody. If all our days were days of prosperity, we would not enjoy them as much. And if all our days were days of adversity, we would be overwhelmed with sorrow. Life's ups and downs produce harmony, like the white and black keys on a piano.

There are times of prosperity, such as Easter season and Christmas season. These are days of full plates and merry making, days when the air is light and the sun is bright. Conversely, there are days of adversity, such as when a loved one is lost or when health is disrupted by a nagging problem.

But such contrast is necessary. Contrast can give meaning. The text you're reading is written in black on a white background. How could you read it if it were written in white?

The vicissitudes of life are unavoidable, yet we can be sure that all of your days are in God's hands:

> *All the days ordained for me were written*
> *in your book before one of them came to be.*
> (Psalm 139:16, NIV)

The equinoxes—spring equinox and autumn equinox—represent seasons of prosperity and adversity. The spring equinox takes place sometime around March 21 and the autumn equinox sometime around September 22.

Job's story is one that displays the balances of life. The book opens with Job enjoying abundance and prosperity, but then disaster strikes, and most of the rest of the book details Job's and his friends' reactions to that disaster. Until God shows up on the scene: Then Job's fortunes are restored, and the Bible says:

> *So the Lord blessed the latter end of Job*
> *more than his beginning.* (Job 42:12)

Life will have its ups and downs, but with God on the scene, it will all turn out well.

Prayers

- Heavenly Father, though I may be in a season of conflict and pain, thank you for your promise that *"joy cometh in the morning"* (Psalm 30:5).
- I declare in Jesus' name that my Shepherd is with me as I walk through this *"valley"* and "Surely goodness and mercy shall follow me all the days of my life" (Psalm 23:4, 6)

18

AUTUMNAL EQUINOX—WHEN THINGS FALL APART

And we know that all things work together for good to them that love God, to them who are the called according to his purpose.

Romans 8:28

What happens when things fall apart, when it seems all your hopes and expectations are dashed in pieces? All your years of labor and investment are burned to ashes before your very eyes? These are the things that take place in the autumn seasons of our life.

The autumn season is not for the fainthearted. It's a time when God plucks from our life the superfluous leaves, the weak branches, the dead bark. As Jesus said:

> *"My Father is the gardener. He cuts off every branch in me that bears no fruit, while every branch that does bear fruit he prunes so that it will be even more fruitful."* (John 15:1, NIV)

From the "branch's" point of view, this is a painful process. To see seemingly good things taken from us is traumatizing. But the truth is, it would be more dreadful to see them rot and decay before our very eyes.

This is the season of life when our pride, our results, are crushed and turned to ashes and blown away. It's the season when, if given the choice, we might prefer death to life, as Job said, *"When I say, my bed shall comfort me, my couch shall ease my complaint: then thou scarest me with dreams, and terrifiest me through visions: so that my soul chooseth strangling, and death rather than my life" (Job 7:14-15).*

Why? Because what's the reason for living when all hope seems lost? What's there to live for when our dreams, our imagined castles, come crashing down? It's a time when we have more questions than answers: Why? When? What? How?

The autumn of life is a time for pruning, a time of purification:

> *And he shall sit as a refiner and purifier of silver: and he shall purify the sons of Levi, and purge them as gold and silver, that they*

may offer unto the LORD an offering in righteousness." (Malachi 3:3)

It is a time to shed excess weight, a time to do away with frivolities and needless attachments. A time when, like the eagle, we soar to the highest mountains and shed our feathers and…. hope.

And while we hope, we wait. While we wait, we pray. The Gardner is at work.

Prayers

- I arise with Christ and I am seated together with him in heavenly places far above the principalities, rulers and dominions of this world, in the Name of Jesus. I sit at the right hand of God.
- I know who I am—I am the child of God, I am seated with Christ. I take my position now in the name of Jesus.

19

SPRING EQUINOX—A NEW THING

Behold, I will do a new thing; now it shall spring forth; shall ye not know it? I will even make a way in the wilderness, and rivers in the desert.

Isaiah 43:19

And he hath put a new song in my mouth, even praise unto our God: many shall see it, and fear, and shall trust in the Lord.

Psalm 40:3

His compassions fail not. They are new every morning.

Lamentations 3:22-23

Our God is a God of new things: new days, new mercies, new songs, and *new opportunities*. That is what the season of spring represents, the season of new things, of bright skies and fresh meadows, of birth and life and hope. Spring is literally a time to *spring* to life.

What new thing might God want to do in your life. "Oh, it's too late for me, Pastor Charles. I'm too old. All my opportunities have passed me by." No, beloved, not with our God of new things on the throne! There is always a new spring season for his children.

In 2006 the painting *Sugaring Off*, by American folk artist Grandma Moses, sold for $1.2 million. It depicts a rural New England town collecting maple syrup in the snow. Grandma Moses' paintings have been displayed in museums around the world, and on greeting cards and other merchandise. During her life, Grandma Moses, whose real name was Anna Mary Robertson Moses, enjoyed great popularity, appearing on magazine covers, TV programs, and winning various awards.

The remarkable thing is that she did not begin painting until she was in her 70's! And then only because arthritis made it too difficult for her to hold her embroidery needles. She did not begin to paint in earnest until she was 78 years old — but that turned out to be soon enough.

What is it supposed to be too late for you to start doing? What would Grandma Moses say to that?

Beloved, spring is here if you're a believer! God is ready to do new things for you. Go ahead and *spring* to life.

Prayers

- I drag every enemy of my ministry to the court of Almighty. Let God arise in the Name of Jesus and judge them by fire!
- I drag every enemy of my progress and destiny to the court of Almighty. Let God arise in the Name of Jesus and judge them by fire!

COMMAND THE SEASONS

Lift up your heads, O ye gates; and be ye lift up, ye everlasting doors; and the King of glory shall come in.

Psalm 24:7

The seasonal solstices and equinoxes represent the gates of the seasons: summer, autumn, winter, and spring. Each season plays an important role in our life, an essential part in the cycle of seedtime and harvest that God intends to provide us with abundance. As gates, they mark *points of entrance* which must be possessed and secured by God's people against the attacks of the enemy.

The way to possess the gates of the seasons of your life is through pray, our most powerful weapon:

> *The effectual fervent prayer of a righteous man availeth much.* (James 5:16)

Below, I have provided prayers and faith declarations to help you guard the seasons of your life.

Prayers

- Lift up your heads, O gates! And be lifted up, O ancient doors.
- My city, I possess your gates, by the power in the blood of Jesus Christ.
- I pull down every evil altar opposing me at the gates of my city.
- I set ablaze every evil altar opposing the will of Elohim at the gate.
- Any power assigned to oppose the plan of Elohim for my life, I destroy your power and bury you now, in the name of Jesus Christ.
- Let all the powers encamping against my goodness and breakthroughs become confused and be scattered in the name of Jesus.
- (Hold your belly) Declare I disgrace every witchcraft burial in the name of Jesus.
- All my buried virtues, be exhumed in the name of Jesus.
- I come under the covering of the blood of Jesus to declare your glory.
- I command the morning to take hold of the ends of the earth and shake the wicked out of it (Job 38:12). I declare open heavens by fire!!!

- I command every evil eye, every demonic eye assigned against me, to go blind.
- I put on the whole armor of Christ in the name of Jesus.
- I take authority over this day, and all the elements of the day in the name of Jesus.
- I draw upon heavenly resources today, in the name of Jesus.
- I confess that this is the day that the Lord has made, I will rejoice and be glad in it.
- I decree that all the elements of this day will cooperate with me, in the name of Jesus.
- I decree that these elemental forces will refuse to cooperate with my enemies this day.
- I speak unto you, O sun, moon, and stars; you will not smite me and my family this day in the name of Jesus.
- My Father who art in heaven, ARISE!! Shake the wickedness out of the ends of the earth in the name of Jesus.
- I set ablaze every evil altar (shrine, temple, coven) raised against me, and I withdraw all my virtues.
- I pull down every negative energy planning to operate against my life this day, in the name of Jesus.
- I capture this day from the hands of evil and demonic operators, and I spoil their works with the blood of Jesus.

- In the name of Jesus, I possess the gates of this day, week, time, season, and year.
- You, my city gates, I possess you by fire!!! In the name of Jesus.
- I sack every evil gate-man at the gates of my progress and prosperity in the name of Jesus.
- Lift up your heads, O gates! And be lifted up, O ancient doors, forever in the name of Jesus.
- I command every ritual and blood sacrifice assigned against me, lose your power.
- Every blood covenant entered against me, I break and reverse.
- I take authority over every evil and diabolical contract or transaction formed against me, and I render them null and void.
- I break the covenants and agreements against me in the name of Jesus.
- Evil yokes (chains, ropes, cords) manufactured against my marriage, progress, health and destiny, break by fire!!!
- I take authority over every pestilence, and I command the curse of poverty to be broken; curses of infirmity and death, be broken in the name of Jesus.
- I loose myself from every curse, bewitchment, and enchantment. Amen.
- I fire back 100-fold every arrow of curse fired against my life and destiny

- I undo every evil word spoken by envious people against my destiny. I undo them and command their words to scatter unto desolation.
- I reject every witchcraft exchange of my destiny in the name of Jesus.
- I reverse every evil ever done against my life and destiny.
- I reverse every evil and wicked thing done against me by the power of the night.
- Immaculate omnipotent power of the blood of the lamb of God, and the fire of the living God, enter into my body, soul and spirit and flush out and remove every evil deposit, poison, pollution, and plantation inside of me.
- Every diabolical priest ministering against me at the evil altar, receive the sword of judgement.
- I overturn every evil judgement passed against me at the gates of space and time.
- I withdraw their armor and dispose of them by fire!!! I revoke their contracts!!!
- I redeem everything stolen from me—my power, riches, goodwill, potential, wisdom, glory, honor, and strength.
- (Point your finger to the sky as you make this prayer point.) Every negative thing programmed into the sun and the moon against my life today, be dismantled now, in Jesus' name.

- The blood of Jesus dismantle every darkness, evil, and death in my star.
- I fire back every arrow of the serpent fired into my life, in the name of Jesus.
- O sun, become my shield and buckler and shake out all the enchantments and sorcery against me.
- O sun, uproot every affliction and evil arrow and transfer them to those who hate me. (Proverbs 11:8)
- Let the light of the sun be sevenfold, as the light of seven days, and bind up my breach and heal the stroke of my wounds. (Isaiah 30:25-27)
- Father, in the name of Jesus, I break every ungodly soul tie, contract, or evil agreement with demonic persons in my dreams.
- I claim every good dream, but I command the fire of God to roast every demonic and witchcraft inspired dream in Jesus' name.
- I bring holy judgement upon every demonic actor in my dream.
- I repackage every diabolical dream and SEND IT BACK 100-fold.
- I recover everything stolen, exchanged, or swallowed from me.
- If I have donated my destiny, I claim it back 100-fold.

- I enforce the counsel of God over the heavenlies, over my environment, job, marriage, progress, and prosperity.
- Every demonic agenda and every evil thought pattern against the agenda of the kingdom of heaven for me, be destroyed at the root of conception in the name of Jesus.
- I declare that I am a child of God. I am blessed, I am highly favored, and healed.

Author Information

Pastor J.E. Charles is the Founder and Senior Pastor of the Upper Room Fire Prayer Ministries and the Dunamis Christian Community Center, a non-denominational, Spirit-led, multi-cultural Christian organization in California, preaching the gospel of Jesus Christ.

His focus remains on passionate prayer to assist with deliverance and healing of people who are physically, emotionally, and spiritually sick. Some call him "a warrior to the core" when it comes to battling demonic and ungodly powers. His dedication to evangelizing, teaching, and preaching focus on a type of violent spiritual warfare. His motto states "The violent taketh it by force."

Pastor J. E. Charles came from a culture of overt battles with generational demonic forces that had established firm grasps of control over multiple connected people. He believes that open confrontation works best to take on the forces of darkness. He sees his mission as a way to teach and guide Christians to make bold, violent struggles against demonic threats. In turn, he will guide them to discover godly breakthroughs within themselves, their families, and communities.

'His leadership positions include Intercessory Prayer and Freedom Ministries at the Well Christian Community Church, a Minister with the Redeemed Christian Church of God (RCCG), and Mountain of Fire and Miracles Ministries in California. People who know him well bestowed upon the nickname, "Mr. Prayer."

Through these leadership roles, he offers insight into deliverance, wisdom as a prophet, godly ministry, and assists you to understand the revelations that affect your personal life. His goal is to align your life and spirit with God's word and power.

The glory of God's vision exists in Pastor J. E. Charles' heart, which allows him to serve the Dunamis Christian Community most fully. The deliverance and healing teams reach out and affect those who are trapped by ungodly forces and held captive by their sin. His ministry and that of the other leaders leads others to accept Christ, welcome Him into the hearts, and live in obedience to His direction.

Pastor J. E. Charles also delivers public speaking engagements, coaches people spiritually, has authored books and offers business management consultancy services.

Isaiah 5:13: "Therefore my people are gone into captivity, because they have no knowledge: and their honorable men are famished, and their multitude dried up with thirst."

Psalm 7:9: "Oh, let the wickedness of the wicked come to an end, but establish just."

Obadiah 1:17 "But upon Mount Zion shall be [deliverance], and there shall be holiness, and the house of Jacob shall possess their possession."

More books from J.E Charles

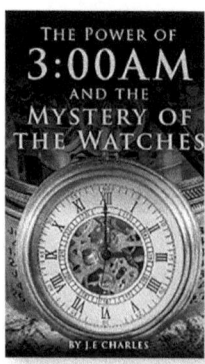

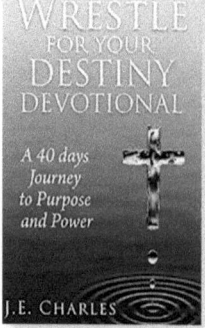

www.ingramcontent.com/pod-product-compliance
Lightning Source LLC
Chambersburg PA
CBHW070447090426
42735CB00012B/2483